WORD EVANGELISM

"Go ye therefore ...."

Matt. 28:19-20

by G.L. Hale

∞INFINITY
PUBLISHING

For "GREAT COMMISSIONERS"
A STUDY GUIDE AND HANDBOOK
FOR
WORD EVANGELISM
"Go Ye therefore ...."
Matt. 28:19-20

Why to, How to, Where to, and When to Share the Gospel of Christ
Sharing the Way of Life

Copyright © 2016 by G.L. Hale
Cover Design by Robyn D. Williams
Edited by Jack Minor

ISBN 978-1-4958-1211-8 paperback
ISBN 978-1-4958-1212-5 eBook

Printed in the United States of America

Published by

∞

INFINITY PUBLISHING
1094 New DeHaven Street, Suite 100
West Conshohocken, PA 19428-2713
Toll-free (877) BUY BOOK
Local Phone (610) 941-9999
Fax (610) 941-9959
Info@buybooksontheweb.com
www.buybooksontheweb.com

Writer's Acknowledgments

This material was originally compiled for an adult Sunday school class I taught at my church in 1998. It is a combination of notes from a book authored by my Personal Evangelism teacher at Philadelphia College of the Bible, Bro. William T. Lewis, and my personal experiences as well as teaching personal evangelism classes, and related studies over the past 39 years. This study is primarily for the individual believer to use in their daily life.

DEDICATION

I dedicate this work to these very special people whom the Lord sent to mentor and nurture me, and teach me the importance of God's Word and the absolute necessity to share the Gospel. I am forever indebted to them for their patience and encouragement. Thank you one and all!

Rev. Joseph E. and Catherine Jeter

Bethlehem School of Bible and Missionary Training Institute

Rev. Timothy E. and Bettye Ruffin Jr.

New Life School of Bible and Missionary Training Institute

Rev. William L. Banks

Rev. William Lewis, Prof. Evangelism

Philadelphia College of Bible

My Dad, Frank, and Mom Rebecca

Special Thanks for critical post production editorial assistance by Pastor Rev. Samuel Butler - Montco Bible Fellowship.

And foremost this book, my life's work, is dedicated to The Lord Jesus Christ.

CONTENTS

CEO

Today, most people are familiar with the title, Chief Executive Officer (CEO). It is the highest, most powerful position in a company.

The CEO is personally responsible to the Chairman of the Board for the company's performance. In a similar way, the church is like a huge parent company, comprising many, many, inter-related subordinate companies.

Let us consider our Lord as the Chairman of the Board of the parent company, He then creates countless companies under His direct authority. These subordinate companies are like the individual lives of believers. Therefore, each believer is the CEO of his or her life and is directly responsible to the Lord.

But instead of being a Chief Executive Officer, the believer is chosen to be the sole Chief Evangelism Officer (CEO) of his or her life! A corporate CEO, can lose the position for many reasons. However, the Chief Evangelism Officer position is a lifetime appointment. The believer will never be downsized, fired, furloughed or retired! Your position ends only when you leave earth for Heaven to report to The Lord Jesus. The binding contract, authenticated and signed with the blood of the Lord Jesus Christ, is the Bible, the Word of God. Specifically, the enabling clause is Mark 16:15 "And he said unto them, Go into all the world and preach the gospel to every creature." In the original Greek this phrase is in the past tense, clearly indicating "having gone already." This simply means that the believer has already started sharing the gospel in daily life, and is directed to continue.

Our Lord could have chosen to use other means to share the gospel with each person individually but He graciously decided to include the believer in the process. What a fantastic privilege! We have the honor of introducing people to the wonderful gift of salvation through the method of Personal Evangelism.

By including us, the believer becomes an essential part of the Lord keeping His Word. "The Lord is not slack concerning his promise, as some men count slackness; but is long suffering to usward, not willing that any should perish, but that all should come to repentance" (2 Peter 3:9). The Lord could do it all Himself, but by including us he gives the believer's life meaning, relevance, purpose, importance, and value, regardless of status, condition, or situation in life. We are all equal, essential and accountable. Blessed be His Holy name!

The Lord also simply could have given us a list of responsibilities and then left us to our own devices to accomplish them by rising and falling on our own efforts. But no! Not our loving Lord! The Lord has promised in the Bible, the believer's official contract, to personally be with the believer wherever, and whenever we share the Gospel. "Teaching them to observe all things whatsoever I have commanded you and, lo, I am with you always, even unto the end of the world. Amen" (Matt 28:20). As a result of his personal promise to be with us, the Lord Jesus has high expectations of His believer CEOs. "But other fell into good ground, and brought forth fruit, some an hundredfold, some sixtyfold, some thirtyfold" (Matthew 13:8).

Many believers are simply unaware of their marvelous position as Chief Evangelism Officer (CEO) and the accompanying responsibilities and glorious benefits that come with it. They are unaware that personal, one on one sharing of the same Gospel that caused them to be saved is His direct will for their lives! It is also one of the last direct and specific instructions the Lord Jesus gave all believers before He ascended up to Heaven. He meant for evangelism to be Personal.

Sharing the Gospel, including leading them to make a decision to accept Christ as personal Savior, is a way that believers can directly cause an instantaneous reaction in Heaven!

Just think of it! Luke 15:10 says, "Likewise, I say unto you, there is joy in the presence of the angels of God over one sinner that repenteth."

Notice that the rejoicing is done in their presence every time someone gets saved. This seems to imply that the entirety of Heaven, including the Lord Himself rejoices! So you, the believer, can cause Heaven itself, the abode of God, where God resides, to rejoice, because of your obedient sharing.

Can it get any greater and better than this? In this life, not only can you please God, but you can cause Him to rejoice! This is living. The Lord wants the believer to bring joy to Him in heaven.

The purpose of Word Evangelism is to help all CEOs in Christ fulfill the will of God in their daily lives to share the gospel. And to make sharing the Gospel a normal and natural part of life.

"The fruit of the righteous is a tree of life, and he that winneth souls is wise." Proverbs 11:30

WHAT IS PERSONAL EVANGELISM?

Personal evangelism is what the LORD JESUS CHRIST commanded all believers to do before He ascended into Heaven, namely to share the gospel with others. It is the direct will of God for every Christian, regardless of your calling in life or economic status. Simply stated, for the believer, "God's will for me is to share my faith with others as an aspect of my normal, daily life."

Personal evangelism is different from other major forms of evangelism such as Pastoral as a part of the church service and Instructional like Sunday School or mid-week Bible study, etc. These are usually conducted in group settings such as a church service and various other public meetings. The methods of evangelism are spiritually based and important, and play a vital role in sharing the gospel with lost souls.

Each time we share with the lost we can know we are in the direct will of God. God has blessed us in that there is literally no guesswork as to what we should be doing in this area.

Just as there are several forms of evangelism: Personal, Pastoral, and Instructional, there are also several methods of Personal evangelism. These methods all have the same objective: Share the Gospel and lead them to the saving knowledge of Jesus Christ. Each form of evangelism has various ways to present this saving knowledge. For example, some prefer to use Campus Crusade for Christ's, "the Four Spiritual Laws". Others may prefer the Romans Road approach, which is a way of explaining the gospel using verses from the Book of Romans. Another effective method is the ABC's of salvation. There are many approaches. The primary thing to understand is that there is no right or wrong method. Each method is biblically sound and will accomplish the task of leading lost people to Christ. The purpose of this book is not to disparage any existing method(s).

G.L. Hale

The purpose of our study is to review "Word Evangelism" as another method to share the Gospel of Christ. Always remember, the best method for each individual is the one you will use!

WHAT IS WORD EVANGELISM?

Word Evangelism places less emphasis on a believer's personal testimony as the focal point for sharing. Instead "Word" Evangelism uses Bible verses as the focal point and the believer's testimony as an option and/or bridge at the end of the presentation to ask the individual to make a decision. That's it.

The Biblical Basis of Word Evangelism

There are two Bible reference verses.

1) "So shall my word be that goeth forth out of my mouth, it shall not return unto me void, but it shall accomplish that which I please and it shall prosper in the thing whereto I sent it." (Isaiah 55:11, KJV)

We are guaranteed by God Himself in this verse that the simple act of sharing the Word of God will always have an effect on the hearer. This is the central biblical truth and foundation principle of "WORD Evangelism!'

In this regard, whether we are able to observe any type of outward confirmation, still the Word is a success and will accomplish His purpose. This is because God has given us this promise in Isaiah 55:11 that whenever HIS WORD is shared it will never have a neutral effect on the recipient. Even though a person sharing their testimony as it relates to God may achieve some level of success, there is no guarantee it will bring results in each and every case. This is because they are our words and do not have God's unconditional guarantee attached to them.

However, when it comes to God's Holy Word, He promises His Word will not return empty: His Word will have an effect on a person one way or the other. Because of this promise, we have an absolute assurance that the word we quote will meet whatever need is set before it. While it is perfectly understandable and a part of human nature that we want to see some kind of outward confirmation of what we tried to share, it is not necessary. Regardless of what we may or may not see, it is having an effect in the heart of the person.

Because of this, do not allow your feelings to be hurt if you receive what appears to be a negative response. Remember, the effect God promised is occurring on the inside with respect to the person's spirit and may or may not be seen outwardly. Salvation is something that must occur on the inside! While a person may show their inward change on the outside, we must remember that anyone can have an outward show of professing faith in Christ without having any inward transformation.

God wants you and me to be involved in the process of people getting saved. Because God wants us to achieve success in this area, he has provided us this guaranteed method that will have a direct impact on the soul. God is no respecter of persons, and He has made this method available to every believer regardless of social status, mental ability, background, gender, race, etc. This means we all can use it successfully when involved in the one thing in life that matters most, sharing the gospel of salvation with a lost and dying world!

> 2) "Go ye therefore, and teach all nations ..... I am with you always." (Matt. 28:19, 20)

Here the Lord Jesus Christ gives us a very clear command and responsibility. "Go ye therefore" literally means "Having gone therefore" In other words, as Christians go about their daily lives, sharing the gospel and the Word of God with people, it should be just as natural as breathing. Keep this in mind, for God's people nothing ever happens by accident. Rather, our lives are all about meeting people that we may share the Gospel with. It is really not complicated. It is very simple indeed.

You are unique, your life is a series of divine appointments with thousands of people throughout your lifetime, one day at a time, one person at a time. Does the Lord send you a person you should not share the Gospel with? The answer is no. There is no such person. All that come your way today who are not believers are in danger of perishing.

According to 2 Peter 3:9, The Lord does not want the person he sent your way, to perish without Christ.

In fact, because the events and circumstances of your life are something very unique to you and different from that of anyone else, you have a special opportunity to present a testimony that is distinctly your own.

For perspective on the absolute urgency and necessity of daily sharing, please just ask yourself, if one of your unsaved relatives today crossed another believer's path, and it was your brother, sister, father or even your mother, would it be all right with you if the believer did not share with them? What reason or excuse would be acceptable for not sharing with them?

You see, in a sense your life is like a line on a sheet of paper with a beginning (birth) and an end (death). Your line has many, many other lines intersecting your life from top to bottom. These intersecting lines represent other people. They may be lost and on their way to a Christ-less Hell for all eternity!

Can you afford to miss this divinely arranged opportunity to share the Gospel with someone sent your way by the LORD? Isn't it really a matter of life and death? And you and I hold the key to life. Really now, could this be the last day for the precious souls you meet? Could it? Are you willing to take that chance?

Therefore, your life's journey with the people you encounter along the way can be your own special gift of sharing for the Lord.

THE GOSPEL

"... Christ died for our sins according to the scriptures; and that he was buried, and that he rose again the third day according to the scriptures." (I Cor. 15:3, 4)

"But ye shall receive power, after that the Holy Ghost is come upon you: and ye shall be witnesses unto me both in Jerusalem, and in all Judea, and in Samaria, and unto the uttermost part of the earth... while they beheld He was taken up..." (Acts 1:8-9)

We must understand the verses in Acts in light of verse six of the same chapter. "When they therefore were come together, they asked of him, saying, Lord, wilt thou at this time restore again the kingdom to Israel?" Their question is very significant. They had been with the Lord Jesus for over three years. During this time, they saw the miracles, saw him go to the cross and die and rise from the dead. Yet 40 days after the resurrection, they asked him if he was going to restore the nation of Israel. In other words, was he going to give the Jews their country back from the Romans? This was a very important political problem with many ramifications, but it wasn't the real problem. The real problem facing the world and every individual is a spiritual one.

The political, social, cultural, economic and physical problems are all important and need to be addressed; but the real problem is spiritual. The Lord Jesus came and solved this problem, and we are His chosen vessels to spread His answer to everyone. Therefore, we should not necessarily expect God to solve all of the person's problems, at the same moment we are sharing with them. We must remember that our main purpose is to share about meeting their spiritual need.

He tells us we are to be His witnesses. We are his witnesses in Jerusalem, which is our local neighborhood and community, and in Samaria, a place where the people look and speak a little differently; and then finally unto the uttermost parts of the earth, or everyone else. He wants us to know that we can share the Gospel anywhere in the world and that we have no geographical restrictions on where we are to tell the Good News.

"And hath given to us the ministry of reconciliation... we are ambassadors for Christ as though God did beseech you." (II Cor. 5:18-20)

All believers are called to be ministers or servants of reconciliation when they are saved. Sharing "as you are going about your daily life" should begin right away and become your way of life. It is what you do. To reconcile in the biblical sense means to change or exchange. Hence, a person changes his or her state from that of enmity or gross opposition to God, to friendship or harmony with God. God does not need to be reconciled to us. The enmity is entirely on man's part. Man must be reconciled to God. We are ministers (servants) of reconciliation. We bring God and man together.

As ministers of reconciliation, we have a spiritual mandate. But in addition to our spiritual responsibility, we have an official status as ambassadors, able to represent our ruler and speak on His behalf. In fact, an ambassador is the official spokesperson and representative to a foreign country with the full power and support of the kingdom or government that sent him.

But we are not only ministers and ambassadors; we are also sons and daughters! We have a blood relationship with our Father/ King. This makes sharing the gospel with others not just work. We are obedient to our loving Father. He is not our boss or employer. We are not employees. And so, our attitude in this regard, should reflect this reality through love and obedience. Therefore, God has given us all that we need to encourage us to share with confidence.

FOUR BASIC - SHARING VERSES

"But as many as received him, to them gave He power to become the sons of God, even to them that believe on his name: Which were born, not of blood, nor of the will of the flesh, nor of the will of man, but of God." (John 1:12-13)

"Jesus answered and said unto him, Verily, verily, I say unto thee, except a man be born again, he cannot see the kingdom of God. Nicodemus saith unto him, "How can a man be born when he is old? Can he enter the second time into his mother's womb, and be born?" Jesus answered, "Verily, verily, I say unto thee, except a man be born of water and of the Spirit, he cannot enter into the kingdom of God." (John 3:3-5)

"For God so loved the world that he gave his only begotten Son, that whosoever believeth in him should not perish, but have everlasting life. For God sent not his Son into the world to condemn the world; but that the world through him might be saved. He that believeth on him is not condemned: but he that believeth not is condemned already, because he hath not believed in the name of the only begotten Son of God." (John 3:16-18)

"That if thou shalt confess with thy mouth the Lord Jesus, and shalt believe in thine heart that God hath raised him from the dead, thou shalt be saved. For with the heart man believeth unto righteousness; and with the mouth confession is made unto salvation." (Romans 10:9-10)

THE ROMANS ROAD

"For I am not ashamed of the gospel of Christ: for it is the power of God unto salvation to everyone that believeth; to the Jew first, and also to the Greek." (Romans 1:16)

"As it is written, there is none righteous, no, not one: There is none that understandeth, there is none that seeketh after God. They are all gone out of the way, they are together become unprofitable; there is none that doeth good, no, not one." (Romans 3:10-12)

"For all have sinned, and come short of the glory of God;" (Romans 3:23)

"Therefore being justified by faith, we have peace with God through our Lord Jesus Christ:" (Romans 5:1)

"But God commendeth his love toward us, in that, while we were yet sinners, Christ died for us." (Romans 5:8)

"Wherefore, as by one man sin entered into the world, and death by sin; and so death passed upon all men, for that all have sinned: (Romans 5:12)

"For the wages of sin is death; but the gift of God is eternal life through Jesus Christ our Lord." (Romans 6:23)

"There is therefore now no condemnation to them which are in Christ Jesus, who walk not after the flesh, but after the Spirit." (Romans 8:1)

"That if thou shalt confess with thy mouth the Lord Jesus, and shalt believe in thine heart that God hath raised him from the dead, thou shalt be saved. For with the heart man believeth unto righteousness; and with the mouth confession is made unto salvation." (Romans 10:9-10)

WORD EVANGELISM GUIDELINES

The Three P's

·   Be Polite

·   Be Pleasant

·   Practice Makes Perfect

Be Polite – When having a conversation with others, always be respectful of the views they hold even if you don't agree with them. Allow them to express their feelings and thoughts. Try not to interrupt and pay attention to what they are saying. Politeness, common courtesy and respect will generally obligate the person to at least listen to what you have to say. This is important because in Word Evangelism your goal is to get an opportunity to present the Word of God clearly to the individual with as little distraction as possible.

Be Pleasant - As best as you can, always try to convey a positive, pleasant attitude and disposition. This does not mean you must be insincere if you are having a bad day. It means if you are having a bad day don't take it out on the person you are sharing with at that time. A normal caring and interested attitude almost always gets a fair hearing. We are people of peace, and even when the people we talk to are upset, we can always retreat peacefully.

Practice makes perfect –– Again, the Lord Jesus states in Matthew 28 "Go ye therefore," or as you are going in your daily life. What a relief! This means we can be ourselves when we share with people. There is no need to copy someone else's personality or demeanor because God made you uniquely suited for those you would come in contact with during your life's journey. The Lord Jesus intends for sharing to be normal (something that can be done anytime) and natural (something that is an integral or essential part of you that just happens). The only way sharing the Gospel can become normal and natural is through practice. The more you do something the better you become at doing it. Certainly, it is not our intention to trivialize sharing, but most of us are experts at many things.

For example, we are experts at tying our shoes, food tasting, floor walking and driving a car. How did you become an expert at these things? You practiced a lot, that's how! Things became normal and natural over time and repetition. The same will be true as you share the Gospel. So work on it right now.

PERSONAL QUALITIES IN PERSONAL EVANGELISM

1. Make a prayer list of the people you have shared the Gospel with. God has honored faithful prayers (Acts 3:1-11; 6:4).

2. When people come to you, do not hesitate (Luke 19:10).

3. Arrange your priorities so that you can take time every day to share Jesus Christ with at least one or more people. Never be too busy.

4. Don't be discouraged — Remember, share the Gospel and leave the results up to God. In the parable of the sower (Matt.13) we are to sow the seed and then leave the harvest up to Him. It is all the Lord's doing (I Corinthians 3:6-8)

5. Remember your appearance and personal things. If you smell bad or have bad breath you can turn people away. Take a bath! Use breath fresheners and wear clothing that is acceptable.

6. In the sharing situation don't get off on a tangent. Stay focused. Avoid the non-essentials.

7. Never argue!!! It is the Word that brings conviction (Acts 2:37; Romans 10:17). Arguing tends to build barriers (2 Timothy 2: 14).

8. Be encouraged by the Word. (Ephesians 6:17; Hebrews 4:12)

9. Repeat the person's name. To help you log it and relate to the situation i.e. Joyce, the lady teller at the bank.

10. Never consider anyone past hope. God works in His time. (2 Timothy 1:15)

11. Remember He is with us. With His strength WE CAN DO IT!!! ! (Philippians 4:13).

What do I need to get started?

You will need:

•   A note pad that is small enough to fit into a shirt pocket that you can use to list each sharing opportunity.

•   A pack of 5 x 7 lined index cards to write down the verse(s) you have selected to use.

YOU MUST COMMIT TO MEMORIZING THESE VERSES ACCURATELY!

•   A three ring binder with paper to use for your Share Log. You will use it to put all your entries in the Share Log, which will then become your daily prayer list.

•   Your Bible.

OKAY, NOW I KNOW WHAT TO DO, SO WHAT DO I SAY?

The question is what should I say when I share? That is a fair question but one I cannot answer. The question is one you must answer for yourself. You will develop your own opening and it will become quite natural to you. Most of the time your opening will be given early during your short encounter with the person.

Example: You are in the "12 items only" line at the supermarket and the person ahead of you has 20 items! The person behind you gives the big "here we go again" sigh! They say "man oh man, here we go again." You say, "I guess we'll have to grin and bear it." You continue, "by the way since we will be here for a bit do you have a minute? Do you mind if I ask you a totally unrelated question?" Remember our rules for sharing. Be polite. Always, always ask for permission to ask the question. This is very important. The person in line will most often reply, "well I guess so, what is it?" You ask, "When was the last time you heard the gospel?" Nearly 99% of the time they will give you some variation of "not lately" or "never." Believe it or not, you may find that the overwhelming number of people you share with do not know what you are talking about.

You then say, or what I say is, "For God so loved the world, that he gave his only begotten Son, that whosoever believeth in him should not perish, but have everlasting life.

"For God sent not his Son into the world to condemn the world; but that the world through him might be saved. He that believeth on him is not condemned: but he that believeth not is condemned already, because he hath not believed in the name of the only begotten Son of God," (John 3:16-18) as normal and as naturally as you can. If time permits I lead them to the Lord.

Carry a small notepad and pen. I introduce myself by first name and they usually respond by giving theirs. I repeat their name aloud in my head and keep repeating it so I won't forget it until I can write it down in my notepad. When I go home I add the name, location and occasion to my Share Log.

IMPORTANT: The names of those you share with become a separate prayer list! At this point fellow believer, I must tell you your life is about to change because your share list now becomes your daily prayer list.

If you share with an average of three people a day for a month, at the end of that time, you will have 99 people on your priority share/prayer list. It is a priority because whatever you're personal problems or issues are (and we all have them), you now realize that these precious souls are not saved and the Lord sent them specifically to you. God is not playing soul roulette with you. That makes their problem of not knowing the Lord Jesus a larger issue or problem than whatever issues you may have.

You will find that by prioritizing, your issues will become less and less important to you because your primary concern will be the urgent need of others to be saved. As a result, your life in the Spirit will be richer.

Isn't this what you want, to become a more spiritual and obedient believer? So does your loving Father in heaven. John 13:16-8 takes about 20 seconds to quote. You see, the Lord really isn't asking for much is he? Our Father in heaven is most generous and gives us 86,400 seconds in each day!

The Gospel takes 20 of those seconds when shared just a single time. The Lord is so good to us. Is 100 seconds a day spent in sharing the gospel only 5 times, too much to ask? Beloved believer, this would be 5 x 365 = 1,825 lost souls that you shared the Gospel within a year! Do the math. This format can be used in almost any situation you encounter in your life.

Try this approach and soon you will develop your unique variation, or if you want, feel free to use the method presented here.

My cherished Personal Evangelism teacher, Rev. Bill Lewis of Philadelphia College of Bible shared his favorite opening with our class in 1980 or 1981. His was, "Do you know the answer to today's bonus question?" I reluctantly tried it, and it was instantly successful and I have been using it for the past 35 years. Only once while in a watch store in a mall did someone say, "No, I don't want to hear it."? I shared it anyway. Tell me blessed believer, where else in life can an ordinary person have a nearly 100% performance?

You may not be good at some things, or good at anything for that matter. But you can be excellent at what matters most in your Father's universe! You can share the Good News! It would be very nice if your boss said: "Well done!" It would be great if your loved ones on earth said "Well done!" But I ask you, isn't it infinitely better to hear "Well done" from your Heavenly Father? "His lord said unto him, Well done, thou good and faithful servant: thou hast been faithful over a few things, I will make thee ruler over many things: enter thou into the joy of thy lord" (Matthew 25:21).

SHARING THE GOSPEL AND
THE MEANING OF LIFE

There are always three persons involved in the sharing-evangelism process: the non-believing person, the Lord and you the person doing the actual sharing. Often, the sharing person is usually the one that is somewhat overlooked. The needs of the non-believing and the role of the Lord are thoroughly examined and reviewed in nearly every instance. But many times the person doing the sharing is depicted in function only. We usually emphasize the process or steps of sharing: the do's and don'ts. But rarely do we really address other important factors.

One factor is the selfishness or self-interest of the sharer. To be sure, the sharing person is not a minority when it comes to self-interest. Everyone ever born, except the Lord Jesus Christ, is selfish. However, when we use the term selfishness or self-interest, we are not using it in a purely negative sense. In this context, self-interest is a positive and necessary human trait, and we need to deal with it when considering personal evangelism.

Now, we do not always show our selfishness. It is there but it's not openly revealed all of the time. Again, and of course, we should earnestly pray and practice to limit as many of those areas of negative self-interest as we can. Nevertheless, we are incapable of being purely unselfish, just as we are incapable of making the kind of sacrifice that the Lord Jesus Christ made on the cross. He was the symbol, the perfect for the imperfect, he did not depend on a response that would result in his personal improvement, gain, or gratification.

As we know, there is deep within all of us a little voice that asks questions, like: "What do I get out of all this? What's in it for me?" Certainly there are many positive things available to you when you share the Gospel, and we need to emphasize those benefits when training people. You need to remind yourself of all the positive things you get from sharing your faith. It will strengthen you, encourage you, and move you to a new level in your Christian life by expanding your understanding of Matthew 28:19, 20.

Let's consider a few of the positive personal benefits received by those who share:

Vision for Life - The sharing person sees the big picture. Literally, you see the end from the beginning. You know that God is holding off the destruction of the world and mankind until people get saved. You understand the ultimate answer for all human beings is that they need to be saved. And so you learn not to be distracted or deterred by circumstances, conditions in your life, or the lives of others. You can then transfer this attitude into other areas of your life.

Clarity of Life - Because you have a biblical vision, you are clear on the issues and importance of getting your portion of the job done. And because you are clear, you are stable in an unstable world, and calm in a world that has gone mad! You know that no matter what happens individually in your life, you are not confused and you demonstrate this because you continue to share the Gospel for the Lord in spite of everything else occurring around you. We may be unclear about many things, but what matters most is having absolute clarity about our role in sharing the gospel. You are called. You are stable. You are clear. You are ready!

Purpose in Life - For the most important question an individual could ask, you have the correct answer. Not just an answer, you have the correct answer. The question is, why am I here? Inferred is what am I supposed to do? This question has baffled and continues to baffle both saved and unsaved alike. Obviously, the answer to this question has a defining impact on the life of the individual. Simply put, we are called to share the Gospel. It is not an easy answer, but it is a simple answer. It is not an easy answer because there are obstacles. But it is uncomplicated and within the capability of all Christians if they want to do it.

Meaning from Life - With vision, clarity and purpose, there is meaning, and life has significance. You count, your life counts, and your specific place in life is important. You have the support and confidence of God himself. He has given you something to do, and you can do it. He has not miscalculated or misjudged your capabilities. Remember, he created you and knows you, and he knew what he was getting himself into when he saved you!

Only the two of you know your situation, but that didn't stop him from saving you and keeping you saved. You are important to the Lord and for the Lord. We may disappoint ourselves. We disappoint others, but let's not disappoint him in the one thing he has asked us to do, namely spreading the Gospel.

Answers to Life - The benefits of sharing are far too numerous to mention. With this in mind, let's consider one final benefit. God, in the past, has answered the prayers and needs of believers through their faithful sharing.

These prayers, for the most part, are usually totally unrelated to sharing. They may concern family, health, employment, etc. Sometimes God answers these prayers of the believer so that their resolution will enable the believer to be even more effective in sharing the Gospel.

Remember, the Lord is the master arranger of circumstances, and sometimes, but not all of the time and unknown to you, he can use your efforts to share to also be a catalyst or vehicle to bring you the answers you seek.

THE BOTTOM LINE WITH GOD:
LET'S CUT TO THE CHASE

We must always keep in mind that when we get saved, we are saved first to be Ministers of Reconciliation. Paul says in 2 Corinthians 5:17-21 that:

"Therefore if any man be in Christ, he is a new creature: old things are passed away; behold, all things are become new. And all things are of God, who hath reconciled us to himself by Jesus Christ, and hath given to us the ministry of reconciliation; To wit, that God was in Christ, reconciling the world unto himself, not imputing their trespasses unto them; and hath committed unto us the word of reconciliation. Now then we are ambassadors for Christ, as though God did beseech you by us: we pray you in Christ's stead, be ye reconciled to God. For he hath made him to be sin for us, who knew no sin; that we might be made the righteousness of God in him." (2 Corinthians 5:17-21)

As ministers of reconciliation, our mission is to be actively sharing the Gospel in order to give people the opportunity to become reconciled to God. Sharing is vital and essential to this purpose. And it is what the Lord Jesus commanded believers to do. The Lord wants us to worship, right? Well, in order to worship you need to have saved people. How do you get saved people? What method to accomplish this did the Lord Jesus Christ personally ordain (Matthew 28:19, 20) and what did Paul explain in the passage above? Answer: personal one-on-one sharing by the individual.

We cannot escape this fact. The Bible tells us we are Ambassadors for Christ. An ambassador proclaims the official message given to him from the Ruler.

There are other ministries and offices in the church, but this ministry precedes, and in many ways supersedes all others in this context. That is, people are not saved in order to be a pastor, deacon, minister of music, or minister of Christian education.

Instead, people are saved to spread the Gospel so that others can be saved. You see, there is no need for these other positions if there is no one to pastor, join the choir, to be taught, etc. You must have saved people. So in this context, sharing is supremely important. In fact, if you're reading this now and are saved today, more than likely somebody or perhaps several people shared the Word of God with you. No doubt other offices in the church are important and essential; however, as in most of life, it is usually an issue of priority. What comes first? What is your highest priority? Where does sharing fit in? What priority does it have in your daily life?

This brings us to the bottom line. Here are a few questions we should ask ourselves. How long have you been saved? How many people do you estimate you have shared with during this time period? Are you pleased with this number? Do you think the Lord Jesus is pleased with this number? If you are not pleased, the thing to do is to start sharing today. Don't wait! Since we have anywhere from 20 to several hundred opportunities to say something to someone each day, don't you think it is perfectly reasonable to set a goal of sharing with at least one person per day!?

Do you think this is asking too much of you? Of course not! The truth be known, we could share with many, many more; but let's start by setting a goal to share with at least one unsaved person a day. One person per day over the last 10 years would amount to a total of 3,650 people that would have heard the Gospel because of you?

Do you think God would have saved at least some of these people? I think so, and so do you. We cannot go back into the past and change anything, but we can affect the present and future by committing ourselves to fulfill our mandate to share for the Lord, starting today!

Let's cut to the chase. The bottom line is that when you rearrange your priorities to reflect God's priorities, you will realize that sharing the

Gospel is a serious commitment. We must make an equally serious commitment and effort to commit to daily and consistent sharing. Hopefully, this workbook is helping you to review, refresh or perhaps learn these truths for the first time regarding the importance of sharing, and one method, WORD EVANGELISM to help you accomplish it.

KEEP SCORE AND MAKE A DIFFERENCE, A REAL DIFFERENCE!

The numbers, or keeping your score is the only way to be completely honest and transparent about your sharing. The simple truth is, you are either sharing the Gospel or you aren't. Numbers are a very important part of our lives. We keep track of numbers for many important matters such as the number of hours worked, money owed, amount of individual bills, grades, paychecks, weight, age, mileage, speed, calories, etc.

Numbers are important in all of these areas, and the same is true in regards to sharing. Doing so will keep you honest with the Lord, as well as with yourself. This is true whether you are a Pastor, Deacon, Sunday school teacher, or just a saved church member. Regardless of your position, your numbers will tell the real story about you. What story do your numbers say about you? Are they a source of encouragement or a source of conviction? Whichever it may be, you are in control. You decide, and you can make a difference; a real difference. If you say you want to share for the Lord, then the proof will be in your numbers. The numbers provide tangible evidence of your real commitment to the Lord in obedience to him regarding the Gospel.

Let's be clear, there is absolutely no substitute for sharing. No amount of ministries, good works, godly living, church attendance or giving will ever substitute, satisfy or make up for you not personally sharing for the Lord. You must decide if you will be like millions of well-meaning and good intentioned Christians that spend their entire lives avoiding and evading the command to share. However, even if you do not share as often as you should, rest assured that the Lord is merciful and full of grace, and is willing to forgive. But is that what you want? No! A thousand times no!

G.L. Hale

When you share you can have the chance to cause heaven to rejoice. The Lord says in Luke 15:7, "I say unto you that likewise JOY shall be in heaven over one sinner that repenteth more than over ninety and nine just persons, which need no repentance." You can partake in bringing joy to heaven! The Lord is giving you this tremendous opportunity.

You matter to the Lord, you are important to him; so take advantage of these opportunities and make a difference. There is no need to hesitate any longer. He said, "Go ye therefore" (Matthew 28:19). Only you can decide. You can do it! The Lord has confidence in you and will help you! Therefore, it's time to get "GOING!"

Consider what he said in the verse prior to Matthew 28:19. Verse 18 says "And Jesus came and spoke unto them saying "all power is given unto me in heaven and in earth." Then He says, "Go ye therefore." You see, you are not all by yourself. He is behind you all the way, backing you up with his power. You have nothing to fear. No one is stronger than Him. No one! The Lord Jesus reinforces the reality of his presence with you while you're sharing in the last verse of this passage when he says, "… and lo, I am with you always, even unto the end of the world. Amen"

You are not alone. He is with you! You can do it; I know you can! The Lord is depending on us, and we can't let him down. He's not going to do the sharing for us. He wants us to do it. Make a difference; make a real difference.

Knowing our score is the only way to know if we are achieving our sharing goals. Keeping numbers can clarify and simplify this. For instance, if you have been saved for, let's say five years and God decides to call you home today, five years equals 1,825 days. On average, you would have encountered 20 to 30 people per day. This comes to about 36,500, but let us assume that you share to one person a day out of the 20 or more you encounter. That would come to 1,825 people over a period of 43,800 hours. If you share with 1,825 people somebody should have gotten saved. But even if no one gets saved, you have still been obedient.

It is important to set a goal for yourself and sharing. Let's say you choose a very achievable goal of only two people per day. Then let's suppose today passes, and for whatever reason you did not share with anyone. Because of this do you make up for it immediately? You could, and that would be fine; but your motive is very important. Make sure you're doing it in the right spirit. Remember, sharing is not a contest or competition, or even a quota system. It is a command from the Lord Jesus. Eternal souls are at stake.

Of course, we should be sharing with as many people as we can. The Lord Jesus Christ tells us in Matthew 28:20 "Go ye therefore." The precise translation is "having gone." In other words, sharing should be done as you normally go about your daily life. You do not have to be someplace special in order to share. As you go about your daily life it will provide many bountiful opportunities to share to people. Keep score and make a difference; a real difference.

Additionally, always make a notation of each occurrence. Write the date, the person's name (if he or she told it to you) or a description such as lady with a green hat, man with Santa Claus beard, guy on the bus, etc. Also keep in mind that every breathing person is eligible to receive the Gospel. Please note we are using the term breathing here in a non-technical sense to indicate a living person. If the person is still breathing, communicating with them spiritually is still possible. But remember to use godly discretion. Physically, a person may be intoxicated but their spirit is not. Many intoxicated and drug addicted people have been shared with in their intoxicated state; yet they have gone on to testify that they heard the Gospel clearly, even in that condition and were saved.

Keep in mind, should you encounter the people described above you can share with them effectively. Sick people, even the unconscious can be shared to effectively. A person's spirit is never unconscious. When you visit these people who are unconscious in the hospital, remember to share the Gospel with them.

This is why using the Word is so important because the Bible says in Isaiah 55:10-11, "For as the rain cometh down, and the snow from heaven, and returneth not thither, but watereth the earth, and maketh it bring forth and bud, that it may give seed to the sower, and bread to the eater: So shall my word be that goeth forth out of my mouth: it shall not return unto me void, but it shall accomplish that which I please, and it shall prosper in the thing whereto I sent it."

It is important for us not to exclude people based solely on their physical or outward appearance. Just remember, when a person is mentally challenged, intoxicated or otherwise incapacitated, use discretion if you suspect you could be in physical danger.

Let's get back to the central issue: keeping your score.

You may be wondering, just how do you keep score? I'm glad you asked. You can use a plain piece of paper, notebook pages, tablet pages, a notepad, loose leaf pages, spreadsheets etc. At the top of each page write the month, year, and then for each day write the names or descriptions of the people you shared the Gospel with on that particular day. Sometimes the people you shared with are already saved. When this happens write an S next to their names to let you know they are saved.

Legend for my daily sharing log and prayer list:

G = Gym, my local YMCA

NH = Nursing home

S = Saved person

T = Telemarketing telephone call or telephone conversation

WG= WG mall

WG SHP = Shopping Center

CH mall = CH

Mall Additional comments:

In 2003, I did not log all the people I shared the gospel with. This is why the reported numbers are low during this time. In January 2004,

I began to document my sharing. Also, I do not log all the people I ask because some of them tell me there are already saved. If I were to log these people the number would be significantly higher, but misleading. Therefore, I only log people that I get a chance to recite John 3:16-18 to. If I'm interrupted etc., I do not log the entry.

During those 17 months, of the over 500 people with whom I shared the Gospel, I only encountered two that did not want to be told, or .004% of the total. And even these were not hostile. You'll notice more entries on Saturdays. This is because on that day I go to local malls in the afternoon and share with the salespeople in the shops and stores. During this time I spent approximately four to five Saturdays per mall. The response is overwhelming. Many people never heard the Gospel before I told it to them. Praise His name!

In my opinion, sharing the gospel is the most mutually rewarding, most fulfilling and satisfying experience I have ever had. I have met so many interesting people while out sharing. I could dominate testimony time during every Sunday and Wednesday services just from the people I shared with recently. I've experienced telemarketers crying on the phone after they heard the Gospel.

Alas, I am ashamed that I was very lax for almost 10 years. I am certain I have shared with more people during those past 17 months than I did in the previous 10 years. I have asked the Lord to forgive me. It is interesting that you can tell where I have been by looking at my log. Also, I have found that sharing the Gospel and reading the Word of God makes it difficult to serve two masters (Matt. 6:24). Whether it is wealth, family, job, ethnicity etc., sharing and studying is a divine re-prioritizing activity in daily life that reaffirms you are serving the Lord and that your home is not here on earth. Additionally, a log of some kind provides a very objective, honest and revealing look at your Christian life.

(See Appendix 1 and 2)

SOULS BUDGET

The concept presented in the previous chapter, "Keeping score," can be easily applied to the local church as well. In fact, the local church is already applying this principle! How? Well nearly every church, regardless of size, has an annual monetary forecast or budget. Usually the church Leaders and membership will meet and agree on an annual forecast/budget amount to officially ratify for the coming year.

The church recognizes and accepts the budget process as an essential planning and accountability tool. Usually there is one or a series of meetings to discuss and subsequently ratify the final forecast/budget after very careful consideration concerning the coming year's expenses.

It is an undeniable indicator of whether the church is meeting its scheduled obligations. The Church body is also periodically informed regarding the progress or lack of progress regarding the budget.

If the budget is in fact, a clear and honest statement of the church's fiscal health, based on revenue and expenses, members can clearly see if the church is meeting its obligations. It is a figuratively a fiscal life and death situation and to be taken very seriously. No doubt, the "numbers" are checked on a regular basis. The membership and leadership are very familiar and concerned about the budget process, performance and objectives.

So in a similar fashion, the local church, can create a "Souls Budget/Forecast!" The same principles for using numbers as a key forecasting and evaluation tool can be applied.

The annual monetary budgeting/forecasting process, is much, more difficult than creating the annual "Souls Budget.". The fiscal budget is the church's implementation plan to achieve the annual goals agreed upon by the church body. Each member pledges, by faith, a dollar amount for the coming year that creates the fiscal budget to meet expenses and generate an excess over expenses.

Therefore, in similar fashion, the church can ask its members to, "by faith believing,", submit and commit to a certain number of souls (Souls Goal) they plan to reach for Christ in the coming year, and then compile the numbers; thereby, creating the annual, "Souls Budget/Forecast" for the church.

The Souls Budget can also be expanded to include the Souls Goals of each ministry, departments, leaders, pastoral staff, and members.

For instance, if there are 100 members, and each one pledges by faith to share with an average of five people a week (individual Souls Goal), the souls budget is then easily derived. 100 (members) x 5 (sharings per week) x 52 weeks = 26,000 sharings of the blessed gospel to the lost, which is the annual Souls Budget for the year!

The formula is: Individual Souls Goals = Souls Budget

Remember, what the Lord Jesus Christ said to you: "Verily, verily, I say unto you, He that believeth on me the works that I do shall he do also, and greater works than these shall he do, because I go to my Father.

And whatsoever ye shall ask in my name, that will I do, that the Father may be glorified in the Son.

If ye shall ask any thing in my name, I will do it." (John 14:12-14)

Just consider, if the church "only" meets 50% of its Souls Budget, it is still 13,000 people!

The beauty of this is the church does not have to wait until the next calendar year to begin. The church can start to implement this process today!

So why wait? The Lord Jesus said, "Say not ye, there are yet four months, and then cometh harvest? Behold, I say unto you, lift up your eyes, and look on the fields; for they are white already to harvest." (John 4:35)

(See Appendix 1 and 2)

THE FEAR FACTOR

At this point, we need to address the number one impediment: fear. There are many remarks believers make concerning their personal duty to spread the Gospel that camouflage their fearfulness, such as:

- The Lord has to tell me to do it

- I'm praying for the right time to do it

- I do not have the gift

- I may embarrass someone

- I want the life I live to be my witness

- It is a private matter

- I don't want to push anyone

- I can't talk about it on the job

- I don't know the Bible well enough

- I don't think I'm good enough

Many Christians do not read their Bibles and therefore do not know II Timothy 1:7 "For God has not given us the spirit of fear, but of power, and of love, and of a sound mind." The word fear in this verse means fearfulness. That spirit expressing itself in the life of the believer is not of God. The word fearfulness denotes cowardice and timidity and is never used in a good sense.

Unfortunately, many Christians are afraid to tell people about their faith. Without telling, there can be no saving! God has decided that personal evangelism, or the sharing of our faith to be the core method by which individuals become introduced to the saving knowledge of the Lord Jesus Christ.

To honestly address this issue, we need to determine why believers are fearful. Did they somehow just become afraid; or is it something that took place over time? Just how does this happen to well-meaning, sincere and dedicated Christians?

There are many reasons why Believers are afraid. However, for purposes of this study we will only review some of the most common reasons for this needless fear.

I feel powerless and alone. The fear of being alone and without power when sharing the gospel is perhaps the biggest obstacle for new and veteran believers to overcome. In Matthew 28:18- 20, the Lord Jesus Christ gives his last command and assurance to the believer before he goes back to Heaven. The Bible says, "And Jesus came and spake unto them, saying, "All power is given unto me in heaven and in earth. Go ye therefore, and teach all nations, baptizing them in the name of the Father, and of the Son, and of the Holy Ghost: Teaching them to observe all things whatsoever I have commanded you and lo I am with you always even unto the end of the world." Since He has all power, then there is no power greater we could possibly face!! It is biblically impossible!

There is no power greater than His, and He tells us we have His power when sharing the Gospel, which clearly, undeniably, and specifically emphasizes His presence. The Word of God! And the Power of God! And the Will of God! And YOU the child of God!

All working together in perfect harmony. So fear not believer, fear not.

The Lord Jesus Christ gives the believer HIS personal assurance that He is with the believer personally for a life dedicated to personal evangelism. Thereby, empowering and energizing the believer to fulfill their God-given and ordained Ministry of Reconciliation. In addition to being "all-powerful" the Lord Jesus Christ personally assures us that He is with us.

How can it get any better than that! We are not alone. His power is always with us. There is nothing and no one to fear. We must accept the Word by faith and begin to tell it immediately. You are a minister (Servant) of Reconciliation.

Weak beginning. Generally, new believers are not told that after receiving Christ proclaiming the gospel for the Lord is now their new and normal way of life, and that they should tell as many people as possible what happened to them.

It is a lifestyle change. Of course, many good churches have new member classes that cover personal evangelism. Sometimes the newly saved member does not make it to Sunday school, or the person may have gotten saved on a street corner. Maybe they got saved during a phone conversation.

No matter where or under what circumstances a person gets saved, it is imperative to tell them to share the Gospel with someone else. The longer they wait to tell others of their faith the greater the potential for fearfulness to begin and take root in the believer.

Discipline. Many new believers are made disciples in an incomplete manner. Often the need and urgency to spread the gospel is not emphasized.

Another reason for this fearfulness is that many new believers never see an example of sharing from their new church. If the new believer does not see examples of older believers, especially leadership, i.e. pastors, ministry leaders, deacons, trustees, or Sunday school teachers spreading the Gospel, or some tangible evidence of their new church's commitment to personal evangelism as a way of life, then they too will minimize its importance.

For instance, if new believers seldom hear the testimony of other older believers about how they shared the Gospel, then the new believer is free to conclude that it is unnecessary.

Over time when they realize that they really are supposed to, they may become afraid or reluctant. If there is no program in the Church to promote and encourage sharing such as a department of Evangelism, family and church annual sharing goals, etc. then more than likely the new believer will think it is unimportant! By the time these believers are asked to share for the Lord, sinful, unbiblical fearfulness may have already set in.

These are just a few of the reasons why the majority of born again believers do not share their faith as a way of life. It is helpful to be aware of these reasons so that we do not perpetuate them.

I ASKED, THEY LISTENED.
THERE'S TIME... WHAT NOW?

At this point, you and the person you have shared with, stand at the threshold of eternity. Heaven is now poised to receive another soul! The Lord Jesus Christ tells us very clearly how important this moment in time really is in Luke 15:7 "I say unto you, that likewise joy shall be in heaven over one sinner that repenteth, more than over ninety and nine just persons, which need no repentance."

The Decision. Here's how you can become a Christian. It's as simple as ABC.

A.   **A**dmit that you are a sinner. You have committed sin, right? (Show them Romans 3:23 and ask them to read it)

B.   **B**elieve that Jesus Christ died for your sins. This is the event we remember on Good Friday. (Show them Romans 5:8 and ask them to read it)

C.   **C**onfess Jesus Christ as your personal savior, right now. (Show them Romans 10:9 and ask them to read it) Insert the person's name into the verse telling them that if they shall call on the name of the Lord they shall be saved. Your decision is as simple as ABC. Admit, Believe, Confess.

The Prayer. Although all a person needs to do is simply trust Jesus Christ for salvation, prayer has a way of solidifying it in an individual's mind and heart after making their decision. Simply ask the person to pray after you. The person can do it silently or openly, but repeat the phrases and allow them time to repeat after you. The prayer may be something like this: "Lord, I admit that I am a sinner. I believe that Jesus Christ died for me. I now trust you as my personal Savior. Thank you. Amen.

The assurance. As soon as the prayer has been completed, look the person in the eyes and ask what did you just do? Let the person express themselves in their own words regarding the decision they have just made.

Give them some verses of assurance of salvation such as Romans 10:13, "shall," John 3:18 "is not condemned," and I John 5:13, "shall be saved."

"For whosoever shall call upon the name of the Lord shall be saved. "(Romans 10:13)

"He that believeth on him is not condemned: but he that believeth not is condemned already, because he hath not believed in the name of the only begotten Son of God." (John

3:18)

"These things have I written unto you that believe on the name of the Son of God; that ye may know that ye have eternal life, and that ye may believe on the name of the Son of God."

(1 John 5:13)

SHARING THE GOSPEL AT WORK: WHAT TO DO

Often at work we are unsure about how to create an environment which fosters and promotes an atmosphere conducive to sharing with people on the job.

It is normal and reasonable to experience some hesitancy and reluctance whenever starting any new important activity. Further, the same is true when attempting to establish a friendly and approachable environment for sharing the gospel.

Remember, the Lord appointed you to be an Ambassador for Christ (not for yourself!). You are the legal, authorized spokesperson sent by your sovereign God into the world. You are heaven's and the Lord God's resident representative here on earth. As you know, an Ambassador operates within and from his or her embassy, which is their official residence and considered to be the sovereign territory of the host country. Therefore, consider your desk, worktable, office, stall or vehicle to be your embassy. It is the place where you make yourself available to share the information given to you by your leader, the Lord Jesus Christ. That's why you have your job!

With this in mind, there are some general guidelines to consider. Do all you possibly can to be the best employee, agent, supervisor, manager, clerk, laborer, etc. that you can be on the job.

For example: When asked to name the best employees, is your name one of the first ones mentioned? This is very important because your work habits, attitude and dedication to your job are in their minds. What impression are you giving to your co-workers and supervision?

Do not forget that even though you are an Ambassador, you are also a guest in a foreign land and you must, as much as is possible, respect the customs and rules of the host country, provided they don't violate the rules you have been given by the person who sent you there.

This means you should honor the rules mandated by your employer. So, in a practical sense we should with equal effort simultaneously improve our performance on the job and share our faith. Sharing the Gospel is not a right or prize we win for being good at work. It is something we do while and when we are becoming better workers.

Furthermore, keep in mind that you are not a fan for Christ; you are not a fool for Christ; instead you're an Ambassador for Christ. Therefore, we should not behave like either a fan or a fool. The dictionary defines fan or fanatic as a person with an extreme and unreasoning enthusiasm or zeal, especially in religious matters.

Though they may mean well, some very fine Christians act like fans. They say praise the Lord, thank you Jesus, or glory to God to everything. It is unnecessary and can be confusing to nonbelievers. It doesn't convey a genuine sense of reality.

Now, it's fine to be a fan of sports teams but be a follower of Christ on the job. There's nothing wrong with this. Just remember the Lord Jesus wants followers, not fans.

THE TEN COMMANDMENTS
OF WORKPLACE SHARING

1. Try to be positive about your own everyday experiences in general.

2. If allowed, use Christian stuff in your work area such as calendars, small plaques, note paper, Scripture verses etc. but don't overdo it. Sometimes the understated makes the best statement.

3. Respond to the praise and compliments of coworkers with a well-placed, "thank you, the Lord gave me the strength."

4. Respond to your co-workers' observations when you're going through difficult times with statements such as, "well, I'm praying that the Lord Jesus will get me through this situation!"

5. Whenever possible, try to build up and encourage your coworkers, especially those of the same sex. This is one area where it is all right to overdo it.

6. Use gossip as an opportunity to give the benefit of the doubt to the person under attack. Be neutral. Avoid taking sides.

7. Make mistakes and move on, it's not the end of the world. In fact, it may make you more believable.

8. Attend, but don't participate. Go to the company party but don't participate in the company sin. Come early, and leave early, but always remember to use this opportunity to share the gospel.

9. Invite your co-workers to your church.

10. Pray every day for each employee by name for their salvation. (It isn't necessary to tell them you are doing this).

SHARING THE GOSPEL: A KEYSTONE FOR SINGLES, MARRIEDS AND PARENTING

As noted earlier, biblically we human beings are both spiritual and physical. We possess a non-physical, immaterial existence. We also possess a physical existence which the Bible often refers to as the flesh.

At this point, it is possible to make a critical error in judgment, namely that the physical and spiritual are equal in importance. To be sure, both are important, but one is definitely more important according to Galatians 6:7–8.

"Be not deceived; God is not mocked: for whatsoever a man soweth, that shall he also reap. For he that soweth to his flesh shall of the flesh reap corruption; but he that soweth to the Spirit shall of the Spirit reap life everlasting."

And Matthew 26:41 "Watch and pray, that ye enter not into temptation. The spirit indeed is willing, but the flesh is weak." (Matt 26:41)

The spiritual you, your soul and spirit are eternal and never cease to exist. But the physical you does not live forever. The physical you will one day cease to exist, perish and die. The meaning of death in the Bible is actually separation. The physical death is a definite and irreversible end of your existence. At death, separation occurs. The spiritual you is separated from the physical you. The spirit and soul provide the body with life. When the spirit separates from the body, the body has no life in it. Your spirit and soul go to one of two destinations: heaven or hell, while your physical body reverts back to the dust from whence it came. However, Christians will get new resurrection bodies.

It is therefore clear that if the spiritual lives forever and the physical does not live forever then the spiritual must be more important or have priority over the physical, even in the daily life of the believer. Herein lies the daily challenge for the believer, which is to purposely maintain this "spiritual" over physical priority. Remember, it is a priority to be established and not a balance to be maintained.

Balance implies an equality in relationship. We are a spirit with a body. Therefore, the spirit should prevail. We must be careful not to live as if we are a body with a spirit, and the body or flesh prevails over us. This body only exists to be a temporary house for the spirit.

Given the nature of the spiritual and the physical, it is essential that we follow the biblical pattern to always strive to keep the spiritual our first consideration in issues of life. Once again, believers should not ignore or reject the very real physical aspect of our lives. Instead, we must always acknowledge this distinction and maintain the correct relationship between them and emphasize the need to keep the spiritual in its proper place.

For the believer, this has to be his or her way of life not a habit, not a feeling or something to be avoided or dreaded. It is a way of life. This way of life must be present and dominant in the lives of singles, marrieds and in parenting relationships.

Consistent daily sharing of the gospel is perhaps the single most important act a believer can do that clearly demonstrates where his or her priorities are in life. Surely we can agree that there are other things believers may do that demonstrate the Lord is first in their lives such as, bible study, church attendance, daily prayer, godly living, church ministry participation, etc. Certainly we know this to be true. Then why aren't we sharing with people and telling others how to get saved? The gospel must be shared in order for people to get saved.

Sharing the gospel, can be a major factor in maintaining consistency in the believer's spiritual life. Sharing can and should be done at all times. At its core is the interaction with people on a daily basis. It communicates the most important truth that can be heard by human ears. No other spoken words are more important than the Good News of Jesus Christ. Every other spoken communication can only affect some aspects of the physical. The gospel is the only thing spoken or written that can affect a person's eternal spiritual condition.

Singles and Sharing

Many single Christians are concerned about God's direct will for their lives. In fact, at one time or another perhaps all believers have thought or sought to know this. This is a very important and defining issue for the believer. The answer will be the spiritual compass by which Christians will be able to determine the direction for their lives. Understanding this will help us to know when we stray from our spiritual course and begin heading in the wrong direction or destination and find ourselves making the wrong decisions.

Seeking God is really priority setting at the highest and most basic spiritual level. Granted, there are many bible verses that give you specific instructions. We are told to give, pray, share, study, worship, love, forgive and so on, but can we say that one is a higher priority than others? Yes we can, depending on our perspective.

So let's keep the biblical perspective. It all starts with salvation. All of the New Testament instructions are directed to and intended primarily for those who are already Christians. For example, only believers are asked to manifest the fruit of the Spirit or be ministers of reconciliation and so on.

Keep in mind, we're speaking of priority setting in your life as a single person in the Lord. Where do you think the Lord would want you to place the most important emphasis? In no way is it being suggested that this aspect of the singles' faith should be pitted against any other genuine spiritual activity. It is not sharing versus prayer or sharing versus Bible study. All are related in some way.

Perhaps an analogy will help make this clearer. Sharing is a lot like your thumb. Your thumb is one of the five digits on the hand, but it is really not a finger. You have four fingers and a thumb on your hand. Each is a digit and important.

It is possible to manage without the thumb, but one's dexterity will be severely limited. If you lose a finger you would still be able to tie your shoe, write with a pencil, thread a needle, twist the top off of containers and so forth. Comparatively, the thumb is more important and should receive higher priority over the fingers even though each finger is very important. Let us say, in the present context that Sharing, like the thumb, is "first among equals."

Everything begins with salvation.

As a single person you have a tremendous opportunity to serve the Lord, especially through daily personal evangelism!! A spouse requires priority of time and attention. Whether you are good or not so good at it, being a spouse is very hard work and takes a great deal of personal dedication and effort!

So, if currently, temporarily or permanently, you do not have a spouse, you will have more time and focus than if you had a spouse. The Bible says the single state is the best because you are able to devote all of your time to the Lord instead of caring about the things of a spouse (I Cor. 7:32- 34). This truth is readily received when you consider that you are a spirit with a body and not a body with a spirit. Therefore, you want to be in a position where you can be most effective in the spiritual sense, putting spiritual things first

Perhaps now or sometime the future you may seriously consider marriage. Just keep in mind your priorities in this regard also. The persons' attitude and involvement in sharing the gospel with others as a life style is a critical consideration.

In fact, as a Christian single, consider yourself exceptional. You are exceptional because you have more time, more flexibility, more potential resources, more focus, and fewer distractions than married people. Singles are exceptional. There are more single people than married people; and generally speaking groups tend to interact and socialize with others that have a common status. There are just more single people available everywhere at school, at work, at social gatherings, in the armed services and so on. The number of singles grows daily. We're even born single!

Singles are essential because they comprise the largest proportion of Christians. You make up the central core of the Lord's army whose mission is to spread the good news which will set free men and women, boys and girls, the mentally challenged, mentally insane, the sick, the incarcerated, the rich, the poor, the good and the bad. It will change anybody and everybody. God can simply do more with you when you are single if you let him. Singles are effectual.

So as not to be misunderstood, we want to emphasize the biblical institution of marriage is basic to, and necessary, for a healthy society. Marriage is good, very good. In no way do we want to imply or infer the contrary. But the simple biblical fact is that the married person's priority is to their spouse, family and the world. Therefore, the single person has a much greater potential to do more for the Lord than married people because their focus and concentration are not diverted to a family.

Dear single person, are you willing to accept your ministry of reconciliation to share the gospel in the exceptional, effectual and essential way as the Lord would have you to do? Do you daily and willingly with anticipation engage in your ministerial ambassador's duties as clearly prescribed by the word of God with joy and enthusiasm? If not now, when?

The question you must ask yourself is one of priority. In your daily walk which has priority, the physical or the non-physical? Which has the priority and how does your priority manifest itself? Is there tangible evidence and is the sharing of the Gospel a priority?

Marrieds and Sharing

Do you have a "More Marriage?" No, not more intimacy, more wealth or more health. We understand the biblical fact that singles have the potential to get the most spiritually out of life as far as the things of the Lord are concerned. But even though as a married person(s), you may not be able to get the most out of it, you can sure get "more" out of it.

When believers make daily sharing of the Gospel a serious priority in their lives, they will almost immediately find an increase in the spiritual quality of the marital relationship. As this can help maintain the daily spiritual frame of reference and stability and bring perspective to situations that arise in the relationship.

Believing husbands and wives should give sharing the Gospel a very high priority in their marriage. Then they operate as are two fishers of men, two ambassadors for Christ and two ministers of reconciliation joined as one!

The relationship can be centered and dedicated to the principle of sharing and leading others to Christ. There is unimaginable spiritual power and victory in a team like this. It's the aspect of living for Christ that can help keep the marriage strong and resilient as a positive rallying point, making an issue on which both parties can always agree. No matter what has happened, partners can always find common ground through their commitment to personal evangelism, which will always help bring things back into spiritual perspective. It can be insurance against allowing things to blow up out of proportion. A serious commitment to sharing helps to keep the big picture always before them and keep a growing, loving, exciting, fulfilling, God pleasing "More Marriage!"

Marrieds: grading your spiritual report card

It is clear that we are both spiritual and physical beings. Keeping this in mind, we should consistently evaluate both the spiritual and physical with respect to the marriage relationship. For instance: is a good husband one that provides and sacrifices for all the wife's physical needs and well-being? For our example we will include emotional needs as well as a part of the physical in this context. Is this all that is necessary? Of course not.

She has spiritual needs that also need to be addressed. In fact, your spiritual needs have a higher priority. When these needs are quickly addressed, they have a positive effect on her physical self. Always remember, we are speaking of relative importance. Again, when we say the spiritual is more important, we do not mean it has to be one or the other. Matthew 4:4 says:" "Man shall not live by bread alone, but by every word that proceedeth out of the mouth of God."

Husbands and wives must guard against being good as a goal. That is, he is dedicated and committed to meeting the needs, and if at all possible, the wants, of his wife. This is noble, good and it is biblical.

However, well-meaning and dedicated Christian husbands can mistakenly consider the fact that since they have met all the physical needs of their wives they can erroneously conclude they are automatically good husbands. Then wives can correctly acknowledge their genuine appreciation and love him for his provision. Great, but the husband should still nurture and encourage his wife's spiritual outward ministry. The same is also true of the wife. She should encourage her husband's spiritual outward ministry.

Of course, prayer, Bible study, fellowship, church attendance and giving the wife all of the important elements of sound spiritual biblical nurturing, as profoundly important as they may be, they are still basically insular, focusing on the individual.

Sharing the gospel, which was the Lord's last clear and uncomplicated command often goes unheeded, neglected or ignored.

Let's look at this a little more closely. Just how "good" is the good of the spouse? You see, even if for 10, 15, or 20 years the spouses are outstanding prayer warriors, faithful church members, dedicated Sunday school teachers, choir members, or officials in the church and so on, yet neglect to share the gospel with others, then how good is their service for God? Can it be improved? Is it good to have done all these things? Yes; but how good is it if over all those years the spouse never once shared the gospel or only shared it a few times?

If you are married and reading this for the first time, grade yourself spiritually and physically. Let's suppose you receive the benefit of the doubt and earn a B+ for the physical grade.

Now about the spiritual grade? When was the last time you and your spouse talked to each other at home in normal conversations about people you would share the gospel with that day? How long have you been married? Are you satisfied with the number of times you discussed sharing the gospel of Jesus Christ together? Moreover, how often do you discuss your children, job, relations, sports, money matters, vacations, hobbies, retirement and television programs with others? How would you honestly grade yourself?

Husbands, do you encourage your wife to share daily both in word and life style? Wives, do you encourage your husbands to likewise share the gospel as part of his daily life? Do you pray together for more opportunities to share the gospel just as you pray about your bills? Just think of how useful you would be as a team. Just imagine yourself as a Christian couple sharing team for Jesus, always having daily involvement in the ministry of sharing the gospel as the common theme of your relationship!!

It would be much more difficult to complain, argue, gripe or be overly sensitive about things if sharing the gospel is a frequent topic of daily discussion. Remember according to Matthew 28, normal, daily sharing is not an exception, intrusion or addition to the daily routine of your lives. In fact, it is the integral part of the Christian's life.

As stated previously, it takes a very small amount of time;

30 seconds maybe. If each spouse shared with only one person per day that would come to 365 people, and if they both did that it comes to 730 people. Out of all of that, do you think God will save somebody? You can begin individually and as a couple. How, you may ask?

Here's the best part, keep in mind sharing should be done in the normal course of your lives. When the two of you go to a restaurant for dinner and it is time to leave and pay the bill, one of you can tell the waiter or waitress, "Thank you. Excuse me are you very busy? Do you have a spare moment? I would like to ask you a totally unrelated question if you don't mind."

Usually the person will give their permission. Then you reply, "thank you. When was the last time you heard the gospel?"

(Or alternatively, "Do you know the answer to today's bonus question? When they say "No," then you ask "When was the last time you heard the Gospel). It is simple and easy to do. When you are at the market together and waiting in line and there's no one behind you, use the same approach with the cashier. When you go to the gym, smile and then ask the members and staff the same question during the normal course of a workout. The same can be done at any other similar location you visit either on a regular basis or occasionally. You can even do it with the police officer after he finishes writing you out a ticket. Don't forget the repair people or anyone else who comes to your home to provide a service. Without the slightest hesitation anybody and everybody that comes to your door should be asked the question.

Also, when you're visiting or being admitted to hospitals, nursing homes or visiting museums, colleges, day cares centers, et al, always be ready to share the gospel God has provided an abundance of opportunities for married couples. Can you think of others? The fields are white unto harvest. Get "More" out of your marriage. Make sharing the gospel the focus and centerpiece of your relationship. Get a brand new **"More Marriage"** today"!

Children

When children hear and see their parents engage in normal daily one on one personal evangelism, they will learn, absorb and hopefully copy their parent's repetitive behavior. Children know what is really important in their parent's lives by what they hear their parents discuss and see them do.

Parents may generally think spiritual things are uppermost on the family priority list, but often if asked, their children will disagree with them, especially if all they see or hear are contradictory words and lifestyle. The children may reply that education, wealth, ethnicity, jobs, status, intelligence, etc. are the uppermost concerns to their parents.

Perhaps, this is what they really see and hear. Despite the fact that the parents emphatically assert otherwise; saying they faithfully take their children to church every Sunday, as if taking the children to church every Sunday is confirmation that spiritual things actually have priority.

Parents should begin to instruct their children from an early age to share the Gospel. Certainly the most effective teaching methods for your children are to see and hear their parents.

Our spirits are ageless. The only difference between a person five years old and 45 years old, as far as the Spirit is concerned is that one spirit is housed in the smaller and younger body of a five-year-old.

At age 45 the person may have changed physically, but the soul and spirit are the same and have not changed. Therefore, the five-year-old is also an ambassador for Christ and the minister of reconciliation. With this in mind, the five-year-old saved child in kindergarten is an ambassador for Christ and Minister of reconciliation assigned to his or her kindergarten class.

The child's classroom is just as much the child's embassy as the parent's workplace is the parent's embassy. Only the location and people are different. Whether young or old, these souls need to hear the gospel of Christ. Essentially it's the same, whether it be a 35-year old adult or five-year-old kid, each sharing in their environment.

When parents begin expressing and encouraging their children to share the gospel and the positive spiritual benefits, it establishes context and provides focus to their lives as well as motivation for life itself. Parents, it will help your children put their priorities in correct order very early in their lives!

Furthermore, your child may avoid many detrimental and misguided behavior philosophies that can set the tone for their lives and lead them into a life of sin and regret. Their focus has a chance to become something greater than themselves, so they are less likely to be so self-centered, self-indulgent and insular. Consistent sharing, along with meaningful Bible study significantly reduces the number and severity of bad decisions your child may make in life. There is also a very strong possibility they will pass along the importance of sharing and having a strong walk with God to their children.

By starting from the early grades, the children's ease, ability and confidence will improve as they enter the higher grades and young adulthood. The outcome of this encouragement and training by the parents will hopefully produce an adult committed to the gospel as a way of life. Consider that the children have the potential to reach literally thousands of people by the time they are adults!

To be sure, it is probably safe to assume that many well meaning Christian parents have not guided or nurtured their children regarding the importance of sharing the gospel. No doubt, these Christian parents love the Lord, love their children and want to do the right thing for their children.

It is often just a matter of what and how you are taught. But whatever the reasons, this is no time for blame or feelings of guilt. Souls hang in the balance! We must get on with the task at hand of showing our beloved children the "Sharing way of life." Let's concentrate on today and tomorrow.

So what if your children are now all grown up, what do you do now? The first thing to do is for the parents to start sharing on a daily basis themselves and take responsibility for their spiritual obligations. Then begin to tell the children immediately that you now understand how you have neglected the great commission and have begun to sharing the gospel on a daily basis as a way of life, and you encourage them to do the same, assuming they are Christians.

Suppose your children are already grown; whether they are away at school, in the armed services or living on their own, and you did not emphasize sharing the gospel with them while they were growing up. You can still have a major impact on them spiritually and for the cause of Christ. Your earnest encouragement may well cause the gospel to be spread by those who have not been doing so before.

Tell them about your everyday sharing experiences and give examples. Just talk about it. There's no need to force anything on them. If you begin sharing on a daily basis to at a normal pace as a way of life, it becomes so natural and there will never be any forcing involved. They will see it is a part of you, as it should be.

However, the child may say that you are too pushy. But often, this is just to cover up their reluctance to do it. Don't let that stop you; you know how your children are. All you have to do is convey your thoughts and ideas in a non-threatening, non-judgmental manner. But don't be afraid to show genuine enthusiasm. My goodness, a Christian is supposed to be excited about sharing the life-saving gospel of salvation. Right? You are simply trying to encourage them.

Also, ask your young children to go with you to the store so they can see you share the gospel under normal, everyday conditions. Discuss with them what happened before and after the trip, and then suggest they try it at the next opportunity.

If they're college students, whether residents or commuters, remind them they are ministers of reconciliation and ambassadors for Christ, assigned to the college or school they are attending. Therefore, they are the Lord's official representative and servant to reach souls for Christ at that particular location. However, they must be careful. Some schools may consider it proselytizing and forbid it. Even so, there is usually a large number of non-students your child will encounter, such as employees of the school and people in the local community.

If they are working adults, parents should encourage them to share while at work, perhaps during breaks or lunch, but only when permissible. Also, tell your son or daughter to get an employee directory if available, and make the directory a daily prayer list. If a directory of names is not accessible, then ask them to write down the names of all the employees they can and make these names a part of their daily prayer list.

For those adults living at home with their parents, getting them to share will also have an effect on their lives. Presumably because they are still at home the parents may be able to have a more immediate and effective impact than if the adult children were not living at home.

Even though they may have a job title or designation, or a specific function on the job, remind them they have been made by Christ to be fishers of men. This is their primary job description and job title. And so, our purpose is to share the gospel of Christ and to give the lost an opportunity to be saved.

Briefly, allow me a moment to share some thought to consider when your job may be in jeopardy due to downsizing or firing (assuming the Christian committed no infraction or offense to directly cause an involuntary separation from the job).

Perhaps we should consider Romans 8:28 in this regard. "And we know that all things work together for good to them that love God, to them who are the called according to his purpose."

It is possible your separation may not be performance related but "souls" related. Notice I did not say Christians are never fired or downsized. But we must always keep in mind that the Lord has the right and power to reassign and relocate his ambassadors according to His will to areas where he wants you to share with people. Therefore, in a sense with respect to the job, the faithful Christian is in some cases really not downsized, or fired etc. According to Romans 8:28 it may not be performance related, but "souls' related. I am not saying Christians are never fired or downsized. But we must always keep in mind, the King has the right and power to reassign and relocate his ambassadors according to His will.

We have to decide what kind of ambassadors or servants we are going to be? Are we going to be good soldiers and obedient servants, willing to receive new orders and accept being let go, with the understanding that the real purpose was to begin our new sharing assignment?

2 Timothy 2:3 tells us: "Thou therefore endure hardness, as a good soldier of Jesus Christ."

Often, the reassigning may involve financial and logistical challenges and cause severe inconveniences and disruptions. But we are assured that the Lord is in control. Sometime, we may encounter difficult terrain and various obstacles while moving from one embassy battlefield to another. But, we are able to delight in the knowledge that we are a part of his plan to save the lost. You must stress this to your children so they will not become discouraged should they lose their employment. But, consider that the Lord may be allowing this to happen according to his will.

Students

Schools, whether elementary, college, tech schools, or graduate schools are abundantly rich and fertile centers to share the gospel. Before we continue, it must be made clear that if at all possible we should respect the laws and regulations enforced at these institutions! However, at the time of this writing we are unaware of any laws in the US or Canada that prohibit sharing the gospel during the course of a normal conversation. So far it is not prohibited speech.

There are two primary reasons schools are an ideal forum for spreading the Gospel: one, students are generally open and will listen to what you have to say. And two, it is also a priceless opportunity for Christians to grow, gain experience and spiritually boost their confidence.

Also, the sooner students begin sharing, the better it is for them. The school environment can be a place for tremendous individual spiritual growth as they share their faith. This activity encourages students to remain spiritually focused.

The question is often asked by parents, "I want my child to begin sharing their faith as early as possible, but how early should they start?" When or in what grade should they begin to share? Keep in mind that sharing the Gospel simply involves asking a question and giving some information. Early on in life they begin to experimenting with their speaking skills by asking questions and giving information. The sharing experience is the asking of the question for permission and the giving of some gospel information. It is a very uncomplicated and easy process.

There are many testimonies over the years from adults who tell us that they are grateful they had an opportunity to hear the gospel from a little child and subsequently got saved. Many parents became Christians because some child shared with their child, and their child shared with them, and the parent ended up getting saved.

But the main thrust of our discussion is to emphasize the great potential harvest of souls at schools and colleges. Generally, schools and colleges will not have the same kind of restrictive atmosphere commonly found in the workplace. Most of these situations try to promote and maintain a culture and atmosphere of open-mindedness to encourage a free exchange of ideas, believing this to be the best atmosphere for learning. Sad to say, we see more administrations restricting the exercise of free speech.

However, it is this frame of mind that makes a campus a potentially ripe field to harvest souls with the gospel. Students and faculty, with few exceptions, are generally open-minded, which means they will at least listen to what you have to say. The fact that they are listening is key. Their response may be poor, but what is most important is the fact you had an opportunity to share the gospel with them and that they listened to you.

To make the point, it is sometimes helpful to approach this concept from a different perspective. The Lord Jesus says we are to love our neighbor as ourselves. Is there a greater manifestation of love for another than sharing the gospel with a classmate?

Or consider this. Suppose you have an unsaved cousin that you love dearly. Let's say one of the person your cousin comes in contact with is a Christian at school. Each day your beloved unsaved cousin sits beside this Christian student in class. Or maybe your cousin comes in contact with a Christian student only occasionally during the year, perhaps sitting together in the bleachers during basketball games. What would you want the Christian to do? Should the Christian student continue to have small talk with your cousin and that's all? Or, would you want the Average Christian student to (1) faithfully perform the ministry of reconciliation, (2) manifest himself as an ambassador for Christ, and (3) fulfill his role as fishers of men and share the gospel with your cousin? Of course you would!

As in the above example, perhaps 99.9% of the time the people will come to you. They will sit next to you, be in line with you, and be in the elevator with you, in study hall with you, in the library with you, at recess, in detention, in the gym with you or in the cafeteria. The Bible says your steps are ordered by the Lord. "The steps of a good man are ordered by the Lord: and He delighteth in his way" (Proverbs 37:23).

He has arranged for people to cross your path each day for you to share the gospel with. He sent them into your life today and trusts that you will be faithful. Sharing the gospel is the penultimate example of faithfulness. Will you be faithful? Is God's trust and confidence misplaced in you! No! He knows you can do it if you want to! The fields of your school and college are already white unto the harvest. "Say not ye, There are yet four months, and then cometh harvest? Behold, I say unto you, Lift up your eyes, and look on the fields; for they are white already to harvest" (John 4:35). Your Lord desires for you to be a laborer in the harvest. Now go labor for your Lord!

THE MALL: A SIMPLE METHOD FOR FOCUSING ON SALESPEOPLE

What exactly is a mall anyhow? It is simply a collection of shops and stores that sell consumer goods and services located in a centrally accessible location. In a sense, this generally describes a mall from a commercial perspective. Although a mall is a collection of stores and shops; because it brings together large numbers of people to a central location, it is also a prime sharing center and as such, it is ripe for presenting the gospel.

There are several ways to effectively share at a mall based on the categories of people that come there. Generally, there are two types of people at the mall; customers and employees or sales people. For our purposes, we will concentrate on salespeople who are often overlooked as a rich field for the gospel!

This is how it works. The goal is to share with at least one salesperson at every store in the mall. This includes every major department store in the mall and the anchor stores.

In these large stores the goal is to share with the salesperson in each department such as shoes, lingerie, garden equipment, appliances, electronics etc.

After prayer, begin at ground-level at one end of the mall and go from store to store, working your way around until you have completed the entire level. Then begin at the next level if applicable. It is important to keep in mind that you want to avoid interfering with the flow of customers at all costs. Therefore, you should select stores that don't seem particularly busy with a lot of customers. If you find a store to be too crowded, then just move to the next one and come back to the crowded store later in the day. Start on the ground-level. Choose a store and share. After you are finished with the first store, then proceed to the next store and so on until the entire level is completed.

Depending on your time and store activity, a store/floor may require several visits. When you go into a store, simply, glance around slowly and walk over to the display table or counter. Very soon a salesperson will come over and ask, "May I help you?" You then smile and politely reply "Thank you very much, but I'm just looking," and you then continue by saying "I'm probably not going to buy today; but if you have a spare moment and are not terribly busy, would it be okay if I ask you a quick question?" Invariably the salesperson will respond by saying okay. Then you say, "Thank you very much. When was the last time you heard the gospel?" Regardless of how they answer, the key is to respond by saying "when I say the gospel, I mean" and then recite John 3:16-18. Sometimes people will say, "Yes, I go to church every Sunday." Always try to use godly common sense. If they say yes in an iffy or hesitant way, just reply by saying "well, what I mean is" and then quote John 3:16–18.

Remember, you may not have much time. If time permits, proceed to share the ABCs of salvation that you learned previously. Always close by thanking them for their time and call them by their first name if you see their name tag. Or, just ask them their name.

After you are out of the store and out of their view, write down their name, date and location in your log so you can add them to your daily prayer list and pray for them daily for at least a year. I would like to caution you against giving out gospel tracts or other literature with the name of your church or other organization on it. The reason being is this may be considered solicitation, which is prohibited in most malls and they can legally have you removed. However, anyone can ask a question and give some information.

Some salespeople will tell you, "I am a Christian. I heard the gospel in church on Sunday. I read the gospel every day in my devotions." It is better to accept these remarks at face value. Say praise the Lord and move on. Again, you're there to share the gospel, not to validate or investigate anyone's particular status. If the person says he or she believes in or is a member of a cult or false religion, then proceed with sharing the ABCs of salvation (referenced earlier in this book); that is, if customers and time permit.

At this point please understand that quite often you may not have enough time to get through all of the ABCs of salvation. Another salesperson may interrupt, another customer may come along and the salesperson, sensing you're not a sale will excuse themselves and engage the new customer and so on. There are many things that can disrupt the conversation. The important thing is that you just stay as long as is practical and the person remains interested and attentive. Avoid pushing hard. With time and experience you will come to know and be able to gauge the person's level of interest by the circumstances and body language as to whether you can proceed or not.

Always be in a spirit of prayer. Pray that the spirit of the Lord will fix the moment so you will be able to lead them to Christ. Remember, the devil does not like you sharing the gospel and wants to keep them on their way to hell. Because of this, Satan will take any opportunity he can to either distract you or the salesperson from being able to meet, and failing that, he will do whatever he can to prevent you from being able to share the gospel with them. This is why prayer is so important; you can ask God to help make sure interruptions do not occur. When you have the opportunity to go forward, do so quickly. You don't know how long the door will remain open; however, don't talk a mile a minute and cram everything in so it seems like you are rushing things through. If you do, it will sound like you are giving them a sales pitch or just repeating talking points and they will resist. But, if with loving concern and Godly urgency, you covered the ABCs of salvation and ask for a decision, many times they will listen and respond.

One person, or several can easily cover an entire mall over time. Two people can work as a team, going from store to store or they could split up with one person starting person starting at one end at one end of a level and the other starting at the opposite end. This is ideal for a husband and wife team. Usually when the salespeople see the wife, they hurry over. Then while she's looking, the husband can ask the question. A few hours in the mall could easily provide 20, 30 or even more sharing opportunities.

Be sure to bring a small pad and pen to record the first name, initials, or description of each person. Never pull the pad out and write their name down while you are sharing. Instead, wait until you leave the store. You do not want to make them uneasy and think you are writing their name down to possibly turn into a manager or something. Also, remember most malls have at least two shifts and some even have three. This means theoretically you could cover the same store more than once in any given day. Additionally, malls generally have high employee turnover which means there are more potential opportunities to share.

Furthermore, you can also go on different days during the week. Often the best time to go is during off hours. That is, on slow days when customer turnout is light. You'll probably have fewer interruptions due to fewer customers. Just imagine, a mall may have anywhere from a dozen to several hundred salespeople working all shifts per day at the larger malls. These same principles apply to large "box" stores, flea markets, farmers markets, convenience stores and super markets too. They are all fair game!

PHONE SHARING-
TARGETING TELEMARKETERS

Telemarketing is big business in the United States. To many consumers, this is an annoyance to be avoided at all costs because of the inconvenience it causes. Let's take another look at this through our spiritual eyes. We are fishers of men (Matthew 4:19). We have been commanded by the Lord Jesus Christ to share the gospel with the people who get through to us. People are calling to sell us something, or we are calling them because of an issue we may have. This is another opportunity for sharing the gospel.

The good news is you don't even have to leave the comfort of your own home. Instead, they are coming to you. Just remember politeness prevails. The key is to politely and courteously listen to the caller first. Never be rude, offensive, or short after they have completed their presentation.

Instead, politely thank them, and if you're not interested then thank them and apologetically tell them you're not interested at this time.

"I'm sorry, but I don't think I'm interested today. But if you have a spare moment may I ask you a question?" They will usually say yes. Seldom do they say otherwise, in fact, it is actually part of their training in many cases to respond yes. Then you simply say, "Thank you. When was the last time you heard the gospel?"

The usual response will range from "What's that?", or "It's been quite a while". Or, I heard the music this morning." Sometimes they will identify themselves as a member of some non-Christian group or organization. You then reply, "I see, well here it is in 20 seconds,", then quote them John 3:16–18. Most all of them will thank you or tell you they didn't know God cared about them, and some of them will even start to cry on the phone. Some will say they prayed in their own way for God to speak to them. Then if they will allow you, take them through the ABCs and get as far as you can before they have to go. Some will receive Christ as Savior right on the phone with you!!! If they do seem to be in a hurry to get you off the phone, understand that in many cases they are under a time limit regarding the average time they are able to spend on a call.

How about our spiritual perspective? What about the people we encounter in your walk through life each day? Is it all random and so-called fate? Or, does the Lord Jesus trust you to be a faithful minister of reconciliation, a faithful and dependable ambassador for Christ?

Can He expect you will be faithful, dependable, and an obedient fisher of men? And because of this expectation, can He be confident He can purposely send people your way to make contact with you, knowing you will share the good news of the Gospel of Jesus Christ with them?

The telemarketing ministry is another tremendously fertile and open field for harvesting souls! It is also extremely easy and convenient. You're in your own home and the people are calling and coming to you. Again, understand that the Lord God is the one sending these people to make contact with you. Literally, eternal lives are at stake. The Lord wants you to be an integral part of this.

Remember, always be polite and courteous. Never interrupt the person until you can tell from what you have heard that their product or news would not be appropriate at this time. After all, they get plenty of negative comments from people, and it is far from being the easiest job in the world. Often it is quite refreshing for them to actually hear a pleasant and kind voice on the phone.

As you know, the telemarketer or customer service person is working and on the clock. Because of this we do not want to lead them on. If we wait until the very end of a lengthy presentation to ask the question you may run the risk of them feeling used and manipulated. You don't want this to happen, so tell them early. Also, let them maintain control and ask you the question.

Customer service agents, canvassers, and fundraisers who call you are all candidates for sharing. We must change our way of thinking. We must look at these phone calls not as someone contacting us in order to sell us something or persuade us to support a particular political candidate, or group.

No, our attitude must always be they could be calling us because they might not be saved. And the Lord is bringing them directly and specifically to us so we can share the gospel with them! This is the "real" pressing spiritual reason for their call, even though they may not know it. The sales pitch is actually the secondary reason for the call. They are usually trained to be engaging, polite and non-offending to you, the prospective client. This mindset makes it very conducive and open to asking the question.

Customer service people want to be helpful. That's what they do, help the client. The critical issue to consider with customer service people is that usually a relationship already exists between you and the company in some manner. This is great because when they have finished helping you, they will often ask the question that is the perfect opening for you. They will finish up the call by asking you "is there anything else I can help you with today?"

Since they asked the question, you then reply "Yes, if you have a spare moment I would like to ask you a question." You can also say, "May I ask you another question, an important question, an easy question, or a quick question." Regardless of how you phrase it just think about what God is doing for a moment. He is extending to you the privilege of being the vessel of sharing the gospel with him. You do not have to go to them. Your Father in heaven sent them to you. Can it get any better than that? What more, do you want the Lord to do to help you in this area? You don't even have to leave your home. Traveling, weather, or finances; none of these are factors in phone or tele-sharing.

Let's be honest with ourselves. Should we really put ourselves on a do not call list? Except for the occasional abusive crank calls, etc. do you really want call blocking on your phone? Are telemarketers, customer service reps, and canvassers an inconvenience, nuisance, hassle, and a pain in the neck; or are they souls for whom Christ died and are in desperate need of a Savior?

How are they supposed to hear if you don't tell them? Didn't someone take the time to tell you? Just imagine, the person calling on the phone is a beloved, unbelieving relative, an aunt, uncle, cousin, sister, brother, or parent. Now what if, instead of calling you, they happen to call some other Christian. Would you want that Christian to hang up on them or speak rudely to them and be silent in regard to the gospel?

Again, if you are a Christian it is because somebody took the time to tell you. Is God asking too much of you by asking you to tell someone else? It is absolutely possible, that you may be the last opportunity for that person to hear the gospel. Your faithfulness to share is a matter of life and death. Will you be faithful?

SHARING WITH NON-ENGLISH SPEAKERS

America is the land of opportunity, and one of the greatest opportunities we have is the freedom to share the gospel with non-English speaking people that live and work here. So how do we, as predominantly English speakers, share the Gospel with people for whom English is not their primary language or mother tongue?

Often sharing with this group of people can be awkward and uncertain. At times the English speaking believer may not be confident that the person they are speaking with really understood the gospel message. Also, sometimes it is difficult for both of you to understand each other. How do we address this dilemma?

Enter the Internet

Today there are many accurate foreign language translations of the Bible. We can use these translations to reach people with the gospel when English is not their primary language. There are also a number of good methods to accomplish this. However, we will suggest one strategy that has recently proven very effective and successful, in presenting, the gospel in their native language.

For instance, on a typical working day driving in my city, I would often encounter East Indian people working in many convenience stores, donuts shops, libraries, gas stations, etc. I wanted to share the gospel with them, but when I attempted to do so in English I could tell that they did not understand me fully.

Language was a barrier.

One of the men in my office was from India as well as a Christian. I asked him if he knew Hindi, the major written language in India. I told him I wanted him to go with me to share the gospel with them in their language. If he could not do this, I asked if he could write, John 3:16-18 in Hindi so I could ask them to read it.

(See Appendix 3)

However, he could not speak or read the language, but he directed me to a good Hindi translation website. I went to the site and found John 3:16- 18 in Hindi. I then downloaded it and then went to the various businesses in order to share with the Indian clerks and asked if they could help me by translating the passage for me. What joy I had hearing them read the passage and accurately translate it into English. They were reading the gospel in their own language for the first time.

In the area where you live, there may be vendors, shopkeepers, restaurants and other professional and non-professional vocations of different nationalities, whose primary language is not English. When you identify an establishment, find out the language and then download the gospel in their native tongue. Then go to the establishment and ask them to translate the verses for you. This will work for any language, German, Cantonese, Urdu, Arabic, Hindi, and so on.

SHARING WHILE TRAVELING (VACATION OR BUSINESS)

As with every other aspect of our Christian lives, travel should be viewed in its spiritual/physical context. Wherever there are people in any setting or situation, there is an opportunity to share the gospel with few, if any, exceptions.

Travelling is no different from going to the workplace, stores, school, concerts, restaurants, etc. that you frequent every day. Wherever there are souls, we must be willing and ready to share. This is what we do!

You will encounter many new people while traveling. For instance, at a train station you may come in contact with baggage handlers and ticket counter personnel. While on the train you may come in contact with the cafe car attendant or conductor. When you arrive at your destination, you leave to go to your hotel in a taxi or bus. Once at the hotel there is the doorman, the desk person, bellboys, and the wait staff at the restaurant, busboys, bartenders and room service. If you're planning on being at the location for more than a day you will probably meet many different people.

The unique thing about traveling is that the people will treat you differently for being a visitor or traveler. They are providing a service from which they make a living, either directly or indirectly. Because of this, they often have a predisposition to please or satisfy you. Therefore, they're usually more than willing to say yes when you seek permission to ask them a question. For example, I always take a handful of dollar bills when I am about to travel. I deliberately chose not to carry any luggage myself; instead I always get a worker to do the carrying. When finished I always give the person a five dollar bill and then ask if they have a minute? I have done this with doormen, concierge, bellhops, waiters, cable cleaners, bartenders, beach attendants, taxi drivers, housekeeping personnel, room service delivery people, and others.

In fact, I always make a point to order something to eat from room service in the hotel after the restaurant is closed just so I can ask the person the question and no one has ever turned me down.

Just imagine taking a seven or ten-day cruise with sometimes thousands of people who are all confined to the ship. During this time everyone is enjoying themselves and the mood is festive and free. What better environment could there be to ask the question then during a cruise. You could have the opportunity to ask the question 50, 60 and even 100 times or more.

Again, it only takes approximately 20 seconds to recite a salvation verse to someone! For example, your vacation cruise or tour consists of 10 days of 14,400 minutes. If you spoke to 100 people, spending only 25 seconds this would translates to less than 45 minutes out of the entire 10 days. This comes to only .0028 or one-twenty-eight hundredths of a percent of your time. Our purpose is not to get "hung up" on numbers. Of course not, we just need to see that our Father in heaven has given us plenty of time to share. That's all.

Frankly speaking, 100 people is only a lot of time and effort in one's mind, not reality! While we're having a good time we can easily devote about 5 minutes a day for the Lord. A great thing you can do if you are married is for both of you to devote a time of the day for each of you to share one to another.

As you can see, you can easily share the gospel and not ruin your fun. Just remember, fun is for the physical and no doubt, if you're taking a vacation, you probably need one. But go on your vacation with the mentality of being on a mission for the Lord. Somebody may very well get saved. Remember to always keep in mind what is most important, which is sharing the gospel.

Just consider any and all travel to be the Lord sending you to share the gospel with someone you don't know in a distant location. You may not know who they are, but you do know you are going to come into contact with people that God wants you to share his gospel with. Always remember that the steps of the righteous are ordered by the Lord. "The steps of a good man are ordered by the Lord: and he delighteth in his way." (Psalm 37:23).

Holidays, birthdays and special days also provide opportunities for sharing, especially with family and friends who seldom hear the gospel! JUST SAY GRACE for the holiday meal and include a gospel passage such as John 3:16-18. Remember, it only takes 20 seconds!!!

Think of it, everyone is quiet and listening. You have their attention. They want to eat. So you feed them according to Matthew 4:4," But he said it is written, Man shall not live by bread alone, but by every word that proceedeth out of the mouth of God."

Try to be the go to person "to say grace" at meals, especially, birthdays, and holidays that will be well attended: Thanksgiving, Christmas, New Years, 4th of July, et al. You may have the privilege of sharing the gospel with people for the first time!

So feed them.

SHARING WITH CULTS

Many years ago when I attended Bible schools, one of the required courses was Cults, which also included studies in false religions. The method almost universally used was "point/counter point." Our reference text was then, as now, the widely accepted and respected, Kingdom of the Cults by Dr. Walter Martin.

The point /counter point method used was to select a dozen or more cults and compare these false doctrines and beliefs, point by point, with the Truth of the Word of God to refute and disprove their claims of authority. I soon realized the daunting task of remembering the details of a dozen of these cults and other groups!

I quickly learned that the cult member I was attempting to share with was usually far more knowledgeable about their group and beliefs than I could possibly be. This became even more bothersome, especially when I began to teach classes on both Personal Evangelism and Cults to local church bible schools. The point/counter point method was a struggle until I realized that WORD EVANGELISM completely eliminated this difficulty!!

You see, again there are still only two types of people you will have an opportunity to share the gospel with, no matter what they call themselves. They are either saved or unsaved. Therefore, we ignore their group or cult affiliation and share the Gospel with them regardless of their position within the cult!

We rely on Isaiah 55:11 "So shall my word be that goeth forth out of my mouth: it shall not return unto me void, but it shall accomplish that which I please, and it shall prosper in the thing whereto I sent it."

All of the cult or false religion's words are empty and without meaning as far as God's Word is concerned. We don't have to know specific details about the organization. It does not accomplish anything and is just empty, often distracting from the ultimate purpose, sharing the gospel with those who want to hear. Just share with them. No matter what group they are in; cults, homosexuality or whatever, remember to base your response to them on the Word of God.

These kinds of non-believers will have you fooled, causing you to think that because they are this or that, you have to use an approach specifically made for them! Guess what, you have it! It is simply sharing the gospel.

For example, the Lord has sent members of cults to me in my daily walk who really knew their "stuff" and would try to change the subject or overwhelm me with their reasonable (to them) sounding false doctrine. I remembered not to be impressed or intimidated by their seeming mastery over their subject. No! We simply state and restate the Gospel.

They may tell you there is no Jesus when they do, you give them a bible verse. They tell you that you need their book "in addition" to your bible, you give them a Bible verse. When they tell you their religion says you must work to get to heaven, you give them a bible verse. Repeat the ones you know over and over if you have to, Isaiah 55:11 rules.

Also, the points or issues they want to discuss, and the verse(s) you are saying may have nothing to do with what they are saying to you!

For instance, a fellow in a major cult asked me, "Where does it say trinity in your bible?" I responded by quoting Romans 3:23 "For all have sinned, and come short of the glory of God." He responded that this has nothing to do with what he just asked me. I then quoted John 1:12 "But as many as received him, to them gave He power to become the sons of God, even to them that believe on his name." He says if I believe in angels, how many can fit on the head of a pin. I respond with John 14:6 which says "Jesus saith unto him, I am the way, the truth, and the life: no man cometh unto the Father, but by me." He says my holy book says people will reincarnate, I give him Ephesians 2:8-9. "For by grace are ye saved through faith; and that not of yourselves: it is the gift of God: Not of works, lest any man should boast."

There are only two kinds of people in the world, the saved and the unsaved, the believer and the non-believer. These people, no matter what they say, what they are or believe they are is immaterial. Either they are saved or not.

The purpose of Word Evangelism is to provide Christians with a simple, yet concise framework to enable them to present the Gospel to anyone, anytime, anywhere. And allow the Word of God to do what it does best, convict the hearts of those who hear it.

"The fruit of the righteous is a tree of life, and he that winneth souls is wise" Proverbs 11:30

Will you be faithful? The Lord Jesus said in John 4:35 "Look on the fields, for they are white already to harvest," and in Matthew 9:37, "The harvest truly is plenteous, but the laborers are few."

WHEN SECONDS COUNT

What does this number, 796 successful sharing opportunities for the year mean? I mean, what does it really, really, really mean? In other words, in terms of the amount of time the Lord has granted me life during that year, how does it compare to the average allocation of time by the typical 24 to 54-year-old American as reported by the US Bureau of Labor Statistics American Time Survey?

Review this data. (See tables) and see the category "other;" that's where my sharing time would be included. You can see how it compares with other activities with regard to time spent. We established earlier that it takes approximately 20 seconds to share the scripture verses using the Word Evangelism method. This would be 796 x 20 seconds = 15,920 seconds total I spent during the year sharing the gospel. There are 31,536,000 seconds in the year, 526,050 minutes, 8,760 hours, and of course, 365 days. My 15,920 seconds come to 4.4 hours. For the entire year of 8,760 hours, I spent a mere 4.4 hours sharing the gospel! (15,920 seconds divided by 60 = 265 minutes. 265 minutes divided by 60 = 4.4 hours. For the entire year, (365-24 hour days) I spent about four and a half hours sharing the gospel!

In other words, 15,920 seconds for the year divided by 365 days comes to 43 seconds per day. What does this really, really mean? It means I had to ask myself a question. "Did I really spend enough time sharing the gospel daily? Am I satisfied that I only averaged 43 seconds on average per day telling someone the most important news in the world?"

Suppose I doubled my daily commitment for the Lord, to 120 seconds (2 minutes) per day (120 seconds divided by 20 seconds = 6 successful sharing opportunities). This would be more than a 200% increase, about 77 seconds more (a little more than one extra1 minute extra per day). You see, seconds really do count! The 120 seconds (2 minutes), out of the 86,400 the Lord gives us each day, translates annually into 2,190 successful sharings for the year!!! (120 seconds divided by 20 seconds = 6 sharings. 6 sharings x 365 days =2190 for the entire year)

My Christian friend, you may say, "What? Are you kidding! Me, share with over 2,000 people in a year? You're joking! You can't be serious! I'm just an average Christian." Okay, maybe you privately do lack confidence in yourself. Perhaps, this business of sharing looks too big to deal with.

Alright, that's what you may say about yourself, but the Lord Jesus says to you and about you, "Verily, verily, I say unto you, He that believeth on me, the works that I do shall he do also, and greater works than these shall he do, because I go unto my Father." (John14:12). You may, indeed express a lack confidence in yourself. But you're Lord and Savior Jesus Christ, who died for you on the cross, emphatically disagrees with you!!! You just read it! Read it again!

"Verily, verily, I say unto you, He that believeth on me, the works that I do shall he do also, and greater works than these shall he do, because I go unto my Father." (John14:12). And again:

"Verily, verily, I say unto you, He that believeth on me, the works that I do shall he do also, and greater works than these shall he do, because I go unto my Father." (John14:12).

There is no lack of confidence in Him for you! YOU CAN DO IT! Why? Because The Lord Jesus said you could! Whom will you listen to, dear friend? Listen to your Lord! You can trust Him! You can believe Him! Take Him at His word! He has never lied, nor can He lie, nor will He lie or ever mislead you. Take Him at His word, by faith believing "...the just live by faith" (Hebrews 10:38). Can you spare a few seconds for the Lord, to Share the gospel with the lost and dying? Because seconds really do count!

YOUR DAILY WALK - GOD'S SHARE-A-THON

As we conclude our study, please be encouraged. It may seem as if you're overwhelmed by the information we have presented here, but rest assured it is fairly easy for you to put into practice the things we have taught you here today. This is the beginning of a new and exciting, fulfilling, rewarding and glorious beginning phase of your obedient Christian life. Once you begin "the sharing way of life" everything will change. You will begin to look at yourself, the world and the mission of the church from an entirely new and dynamic perspective.

Your new, renewed or corrected priorities will have a direct impact on the eternal future of many souls.

Here are some closing truths to keep before you; the Bible says in Psalm 37:23 "the steps of a good man (person) are ordered by the Lord." You are unique. There is only one of you, and there will never be another. In a manner of speaking, you are so special to the Lord that he broke the mold after you were created.

You have a unique, one-of-a-kind walk each day. Each day of your life is different from all the other days that went before and is different from the same day of everyone else on the planet.

Every day is very important because it will lead you for a brief precious moment into the life of another person. When this happens, what will you do with this precious moment? God from heaven has orchestrated with godly precision the exact second when your life will intersect that of another person, a person for whom Christ died.

The Lord has entrusted you with that precise moment, not your neighbor, not your pastor, not your spouse. But will you be faithful to share the gospel? Can God depend on you? We must all ask this question of ourselves each day of our lives.

The Lord Jesus said in Matthew 28 "Go ye therefore..." which means "having gone therefore." Just share as you're going through every day of your life. Indeed, the steps in your daily life may take you down paths that may be painful.

But probably your path most of the time will be during the good days. Whether good or not so good days, always be consistent. Share the gospel on both the good and the bad days. Share when you feel great and when your heart is breaking. If you're still breathing and talking, share the gospel no matter how you feel. Whether you're up, down, sideways, happy or sad, still share.

Your life is made up of individual daily walks; each lived one at a time. You cannot relive them once they are gone. The beginning or starting point of our life we call birth. There is also an ending time on earth we call death. We cannot control the dates for either of these two times, but what we do between these two events is vital and important. The only time you will ever have to commit to the opportunity to sharing the gospel with precious souls for whom Christ died is between these two events. Except for his use of angels, God does not use supernatural beings or people sent from heaven to reach the lost.) You are the vessel God has chosen for this vital task.

And so let us close with:

"Rejoice in the Lord in the always, and again I say Rejoice." (Phil 4:4)

Epilogue

As I close this, the first installment of the **Word Evangelism** series (the next

will be a similar study guide, **"Follow Up"-the undiscovered territory!**), allow me to apologize to all that read this work. I openly admit that I am but dust and because of this I may have unintentionally, by inference, implication, illustration, presentation or otherwise offended.

All I ask is for your forgiveness and to charge it to my <u>head and not my heart</u>!

Finally, in Luke 17: 7-10, the Lord Jesus Christ, accurately and honestly describes my attitude towards myself.

"But which of you having a servant plowing or feeding cattle, will say unto him by and by, when he is come from the field, Go and sit down to meat?

And will not rather say unto him, Make ready wherewith I may sup, and gird thyself, and serve me, till I have eaten and drunken, and afterward thou shalt eat and drink?

Doth he thank that servant because he did the things that were commanded him? I think not.

So likewise ye when ye shall have done all those things which are commanded you, say, We are unprofitable servants: we have done that which was our duty to do."

Until the next time.... 3 John 2

"Beloved, I wish above all things that thou mayest prosper and be in health, even as thy soul prospereth".

Thank you for your time,

Your unprofitable servant

G.L.Hale

Appendix 1
Witnessing Log

2003	Witnessed	Saved	No.	Date	Name	Status	Description
			1	2/05/03	Art	G	a guy in the / ... YMCA Gym
			2	2/07/03	Jerry	G	same as above
Feb-03	4	1	3	2/22/03	Terry "Got saved today"	G	runs the "Y" men's basketball league
			4	2/21/03	Deven	G	same as above- senior in high school
			5	3/17/03	Rob	G	same as above-adult
Mar-03	2	1	6	3/23/03	Fred	G	same as above- 2 time NCAA weightlifting champ
			7	3/04/03	John	G	same as above- life guard at the pool in the "Y"
			8	4/13/03	Malik	G	same as above, he is very respectful to the message
			9	4/17/03	Male teenager	G	Teenager in gym whose father recently died. He is still hurting
			10	4/19/03	Tom Washington	NH	His father is on the same floor as my mom in the nursing home
			11	4/22/03	Lady	NH	One of the ladies on moms floor
			12	4/23/03	Bruce	O	Staff person in the fitness center in the gym
			13	4/24/03	Young lady	NH	One of the young wonmen that work on moms floor
			14	4/27/03	Tall guy- in the gym	G	Basket baller from the gym
			15	4/29/03	TV guy- in the gym		Call him TV guy because he bought a $2700 TV
Apr-03	10	2	16	4/30/03	Danielle		V_____ undergrad and friend/business associate
			17	5/11/03	John	G	His Younger brother was killed in 2000
			18	5/13/03	Miss Mary	NH	Miss Mary is a resident on mom's floor
			19	5/20/03	Young man in the Gym Parking	S	Saved . St. junior waiting for his girl friend
			20	5/24/03	Steve	G	He comes to the gym
May-03	4	1	21	6/09/03	Jonathan	G	same as above
			22	6/11/03	Marcus	G	same as above
			23	6/24/03	Dave	G	same as above
			24	6/30/03	Tom	NH	Tom was next door to mom rehabilitating
Jun-03	4		25	7/6/03	Ump		Ump volunteered to fix ... in the dentist's parking lot
			26	7/12/03	Darryl		He was in the IRS office in ... with his 4 little kids
			27	7/22/03	Elder Jones	G/S	Elder Jones comes to the gym
			28	7/29/03	Young, Door man at the Westin	S	This young man is a member at C ... Baptist church
Jul-03	6	3	29	7/30/03	Keith Hart	S	Keith comes to the gym
			30	7/31/03	Larry	G	He works for / ... gym
			31	8/10/03	Kenny	G	He formerly lived in / ... Township
			32	8/11/03	Ralf	G/S	He used to come faithfully, haven't seen him in several months
			33	8/23/03	Sam	G/S	He comes to the gym
			34	8/25/03	teenager on a bike in the park		I saw him on a bike in / ... Park
Aug-03	5	4	35	8/27/03	Tyler	G	He is in the 12th grade at ... high School
			36	9/07/03	Nick	G	He is well educated and wants to talk about spiritual things
			37	9/09/03	Bill	G/S	He came to the gym
			38	9/16/03	Chris	G/S	He is a 4th grade teacher in Philly
			39	9/17/03	Tim	G/S	He attends / ... Presbyterian
			40	9/22/03	Mike	O	Goes to church in the area

#	Date	Name		Description
2	4-Jan-2005	Monica	T	Monica is a counter person at a local Florist
3	10-Jan-2005	Christina	T	Christina is a customer service rep for my new mortgage Company
4	11-Jan-2005	Courtney	T	Courtney is a customer sewrvice rep for my pager company
5	12-Jan-2005	Kerwin	G	Kerwin is Hatian
6	12-Jan-2005	Jacques	G	Jacques is Kerwin's friend. Jacques is Hatian also
7	13-Jan-2005	Tracy	T	Tracy is a telemarketer for my chiropracter
8	13-Jan-2005	Kimberly		Kimberly is a sales person in the Vitamin store
9	17-Jan-2005	Dr. Larry		Dr. Larry is my Gastroenterologist. I …
10	17-Jan-2005	Mike		Mike came to the church looking for the Pastor. Malcolm spoke to him
11	20-Jan-2005	Bob		Bob is a very active wheelchair bound resident at Mom's nursing home
12	27-Jan-2005	Ron		Ron is a teenager working the steak and hoagie shop. He likes the Funkad
13	27-Jan-2005	Corey		Corey works with Ron -see above
14	27-Jan-2005	Dave		Dave wa a drunk in the steak and haogie shop- see above
15	29-Jan-2005	Brian	G	Brian is Catholic
16	31-Jan-2005	Brenda		Brenda works at Home Depot. She is a Jehovahs' Witness. Her daughter c
17	1-Feb-2005	Sid J.	T	Sid is a telemarketer for Nova mortgage
18	2-Feb-2005	Joe		Joe works for heating company that fixed my furnace
19	2-Feb-2005	Josh	G	Josh is in 8th grade doing comm. Svc He is moving to Georgia.
20	3-Feb-2005	Linda		Linda is a nurses aide on Mom's floor
21	3-Feb-2005	Ms. Connie		Ms. Connie is a resident on Mom's floor
22	4-Feb-2005	Taki		I jumped Taki's yellow sports car in front of the bank
23	4-Feb-2005	Tarik		Tarik works in a gas station. He is Egyptian
24	7-Feb-2005	Chris		Chris works in the steak and … shop
25	8-Feb-2005	Rudi		Rudi works for Hilton Hotels
26	8-Feb-2005	Bob	G	Bob is separated from his wife and is about to start divorce proceedings
27	14-Feb-2005	Ashley	T	Ashley is a customer svc. Rep for pager company
28	14-Feb-2005	Mile H.	T	Mike works for Embassy Suites Hotel in NYC
29	16-Feb-2005	Chris	G	Chris was in the Gym
30	17-Feb-2005	Peter		Peter asked me for directions in the lobby of Mom's nursing home
31	17-Feb-2005	Be	T	Be is a Hotel reservationist
32	22-Feb-2005	Dee	T	Dee makes the appointments for my colonoscopy
33	23-Feb-2005	Ben	T	Ben is a telemarketer for Novastar Mortgage
34	25-Feb-2005	Dave		Dave works in an Eckerd's Drug store
35	25-Feb-2005	Maintenace man		There was a maintenace man in Mom's room
36	28-Feb-2005	Dr. John		Dr. John was the anesthesiologist for my colonoscopy
37	28-Feb-2005	Suzzane		Suzzanne was the medical assistant for my colonoscopy
38	28-Feb-2005	Dr. Nguyen		Dr. Nguyen was the emergency room Doctor when My Mom was
39				
40				

Feb-05 22

796

Appendix 2
Witnessing Graph

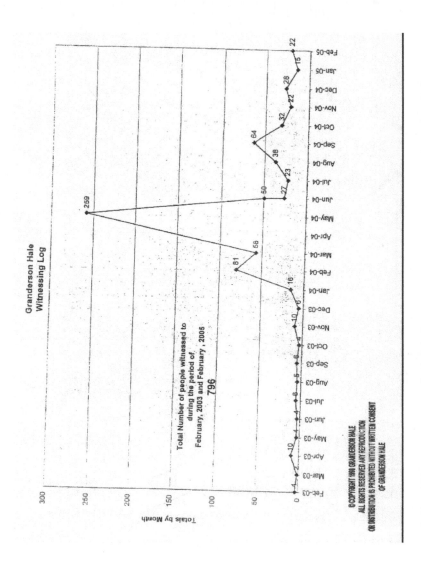

Granderson Hale
Witnessing Log

Totals by Month

Total Number of people witnessed to
during the period of
February, 2003 and February, 2005
796

Appendix 3
Hindi Translation
John 2:4-3:35

खत्म हो गया, तो यीशु की माँ ने कहा, "उनके पास अब और दाखरस नहीं है।"

⁴यीशु ने उससे कहा, "यह तू मुझसे क्यों कह रही है? मेरा समय अभी नहीं आया।"

⁵फिर उसकी माता ने सेवकों से कहा, "वही करो जो तुमसे यह कहता है।" ⁶वहाँ पानी भरने के पत्थर के छह मटके रखे थे। ये मटके कैसे ही थे जैसे यहूदी पवित्र स्नान के लिये काम में लाते थे। हर मटके में कोई बीस से तीस गैलन तक पानी आता था।

⁷यीशु ने सेवकों से कहा, "मटकों को पानी से भर दो।" और सेवकों ने मटकों को लबालब भर दिया।

⁸फिर उसने उनसे कहा, "अब थोड़ा बाहर निकालो, और दावत का इन्तजाम कर रहे प्रधान के पास उसे ले जाओ।" और वे उसे ले गये।

⁹फिर दावत के प्रबन्धकर्ता ने उस पानी को चखा जो दाखरस बन गया था। उसे पता ही नहीं चला कि वह दाखरस कहाँ से आया। पर उन सेवकों को इसका पता था जिन्होंने पानी निकाला था। फिर दावत के प्रबन्धक ने दूल्हे को बुलाया ¹⁰और उससे कहा, "हर कोई पहले बढ़िया दाखरस परोसता है और जब मेहमान काफ़ी तृप्त हो चुकते हैं तो फिर घटिया। पर तुमने तो उत्तम दाखरस अब तक बचा रखा है!"

¹¹यीशु ने गलील के काना में यह पहला आश्चर्यकर्म करके अपनी महिमा प्रकट की। जिससे उसके शिष्यों ने उसमें विश्वास किया।

यीशु मन्दिर में

¹²इसके बाद यीशु अपनी माता, भाइयों और शिष्यों के साथ कफरनहूम चला गया जहाँ वे कुछ दिन ठहरे। ¹³यहूदियों का फसह पर्व नजदीक था। इसलिये यीशु यरूशलेम चला गया। ¹⁴वहाँ मन्दिर में यीशु ने देखा कि लोग मवेशियों, भेड़ों और कबूतरों की बिक्री कर रहे हैं और सिक्के बदलने वाले सौदागर अपनी गद्दियों पर बैठे हैं। ¹⁵इसलिए उसने रस्सियों का एक कोड़ा बनाया और सबको, मवेशियों और भेड़ों समेत, बाहर खदेड़ दिया। मुद्रा बदलने वालों के सिक्के उड़ेल दिये और उनकी चौकियाँ पलट दीं। ¹⁶कबूतर बेचने वालों से उसने कहा, "इन्हें यहाँ से बाहर ले जाओ। मेरे परमपिता के घर को बाजार मत बनाओ।"

¹⁷इस पर उसके शिष्यों को याद आया कि शास्त्रों में लिखा है:

"तेरे घर के लिये मेरी लगन मुझे खा डालेगी।"
भजन संहिता 69:9

¹⁸जवाब में यहूदियों ने यीशु से कहा, "तू हमें कौन सा अद्भुत चिह्न दिखा सकता है, जिससे तू जो कुछ कर रहा है, उसका तू अधिकारी है यह साबित हो सके?"

¹⁹यीशु ने उन्हें जवाब में कहा, "इस मन्दिर को गिरा दो और मैं तीन दिन के भीतर इसे फिर बना दूँगा।"

²⁰इस पर यहूदी बोले, "इस मन्दिर को बनाने में छियालीस साल लगे थे, और तू इसे तीन दिन में बनाने जा रहा है?"

²¹(किन्तु अपनी बात में जिस मन्दिर की चर्चा यीशु ने की थी वह उसका अपना ही शरीर था। ²²आगे चलकर जब वह मौत के बाद फिर जी उठा तो उसके अनुयायियों को याद आया कि यीशु ने यह कहा था, और शास्त्रों पर और यीशु के शब्दों पर विश्वास किया।)

²³फसह के त्योहार के दिनों जब यीशु यरूशलेम में था, बहुत से लोगों ने उसके अद्भुत चिह्नों और कर्मों को देखकर उसमें विश्वास किया। ²⁴किन्तु यीशु ने अपने आपको उनके भरोसे नहीं छोड़ा, क्योंकि वह सब लोगों को जानता था। ²⁵उसे इस बात की कोई जरूरत नहीं थी कि कोई आकर उसे लोगों के बारे में बताए, क्योंकि लोगों के मन में क्या है, इसे वह जानता था।

यीशु और नीकुदेमुस

³ वहाँ फरीसियों का एक आदमी था जिसका नाम था नीकुदेमुस। वह यहूदियों का नेता था। ²वह यीशु के पास रात में आया और उससे बोला, "हे गुरु, हम जानते हैं कि तू गुरु है और परमेश्वर की ओर से आया है, क्योंकि ऐसे आश्चर्यकर्म जैसे तू करता है परमेश्वर की सहायता के बिना कोई नहीं कर सकता।"

³जवाब में यीशु ने उससे कहा, "सत्यसत्य, मैं तुम्हें बताता हूँ, यदि कोई व्यक्ति नये सिरे से जन्म न ले तो वह परमेश्वर के राज्य को नहीं देख सकता।"

⁴नीकुदेमुस ने उससे कहा, "कोई आदमी बूढ़ा हो जाने के बाद फिर जन्म कैसे ले सकता है? निश्चय ही वह अपनी माँ की कोख में प्रवेश करके दुबारा तो जन्म ले नहीं सकता!"

⁵यीशु ने जवाब दिया, "सच्चाई तुम्हें मैं बताता हूँ। यदि कोई आदमी जल और आत्मा से जन्म नहीं लेता तो वह परमेश्वर के राज्य में प्रवेश नहीं पा सकता। ⁶माँस से केवल माँस ही पैदा होता है; और जो आत्मा से उत्पन्न हो वह आत्मा है। ⁷मैंने तुमसे जो कहा है उस पर आश्चर्य मत करो, 'तुम्हें नये सिरे से जन्म लेना ही होगा।' ⁸हवा जिधर बहती है, उधर बहती है। तुम उसकी आवाज़ सुन सकते हो। किन्तु तुम यह नहीं जान सकते कि वह कहाँ से आ रही है, और कहाँ को जा रही है। आत्मा से जन्म हुआ हर व्यक्ति भी ऐसा ही है।"

⁹जवाब में नीकुदेमुस ने उससे कहा, "यह कैसे हो सकता है?"

¹⁰यीशु ने उसे जवाब देते हुए कहा, "तुम इस्राएलियों के गुरु हो फिर भी यह नहीं जानते? ¹¹मैं तुम्हें सच्चाई बताता हूँ, हम जो जानते हैं, वही बोलते हैं। और वही बताते हैं जो हमने देखा है, पर तुम लोग जो हम कहते हैं उसे स्वीकार नहीं करते। ¹²मैंने तुम्हें धरती की बातें बतायीं और तुमने उन पर विश्वास नहीं किया इसलिये अगर मैं स्वर्ग की बातें बताऊँ तो तुम पर कैसे विश्वास करोगे? ¹³स्वर्ग में ऊपर कोई नहीं गया, सिवाय उसके, जो स्वर्ग से उतर कर आया है–यानी मानव-पुत्र।

¹⁴जैसे मूसा ने रेगिस्तान में साँप को ऊपर उठा लिया था, वैसे ही मानव-पुत्र भी ऊपर उठा लिया जायेगा ¹⁵ताकि वे सब जो उसमें विश्वास करते हैं, अन्नत जीवन पा सकें।"

¹⁶परमेश्वर को जगत से इतना प्रेम था कि उसने अपने एकमात्र पुत्र को दे दिया, ताकि हर वह आदमी जो उसमें विश्वास रखता है, नष्ट न हो जाये बल्कि उसे अन्नत जीवन मिल जाये। ¹⁷परमेश्वर ने अपने बेटे को जगत में इसलिये नहीं भेजा कि वह दुनिया की अपराधी ठहराये बल्कि उसे इसलिये भेजा कि उसके द्वारा दुनिया का उद्धार हो। ¹⁸जो उसमें विश्वास रखता है उसे दोषी न ठहराया जाय पर जो उसमें विश्वास नहीं रखता, उसे दोषी ठहराया जा चुका है क्योंकि उसने परमेश्वर के एकमात्र पुत्र के नाम में विश्वास नहीं रखा है। ¹⁹इस निर्णय का आधार यह है कि ज्योति इस दुनिया में आ चुकी है पर ज्योति के बजाय लोग अंधेरे को अधिक महत्व देते हैं। क्योंकि उनके कार्य बुरे हैं। ²⁰हर वह आदमी जो पाप करता है ज्योति से घृणा रखता है और ज्योति के नज़दीक नहीं आता ताकि उसके पाप उजागर न हो जायें। ²¹पर वह जो सत्य पर चलता है, ज्योति के निकट आता है ताकि यह प्रकट हो जाये कि उसके कर्म परमेश्वर के द्वारा कराये गये हैं।

यूहन्ना द्वारा यीशु का बपतिस्मा

²²इसके बाद यीशु अपने अनुयायियों के साथ यहूदिया के इलाके में चला गया। वहाँ उनके साथ ठहर कर, वह लोगों को बपतिस्मा देने लगा। ²³वहीं शालेम के पास ऐनोन में यूहन्ना भी बपतिस्मा दिया करता था क्योंकि वहाँ पानी बहुतायत में था। लोग वहाँ आते और बपतिस्मा लेते थे। ²⁴(यूहन्ना को अभी तक बंदी नहीं बनाया गया था।)

²⁵अब यूहन्ना के कुछ शिष्यों और एक यहूदी के बीच स्वच्छताकरण को लेकर बहस छिड़ गयी। ²⁶इसलिये वे यूहन्ना के पास आये और बोले, "हे रब्बी, जो व्यक्ति यरदन के उस पार तेरे साथ था और जिसके बारे में तूने बताया था, वही लोगों को बपतिस्मा दे रहा है, और हर आदमी उसके पास जा रहा है।"

²⁷जवाब में यूहन्ना ने कहा, "किसी आदमी को तब तक कुछ नहीं मिल सकता जब तक वह उसे स्वर्ग से न दिया गया हो। ²⁸तुम सब गवाह हो कि मैंने कहा था मैं मसीह नहीं हूँ बल्कि मैं तो उससे पहले भेजा गया हूँ। ²⁹दूल्हा वही है जिसे दुल्हन मिलती है। पर दूल्हे का मित्र जो खड़ा रहता है और उसकी अगुवाई में जब दूल्हे की आवाज़ को सुनता है, तो बहुत खुश होता है। मेरी यही खुशी अब पूरी हुई है। ³⁰अब निश्चित है कि उसकी महिमा बढ़े और मेरी घटे!

वह जो स्वर्ग से उतरा

³¹जो ऊपर से आता है वह सबसे महान् है। वह जो धरती से है, धरती से जुड़ा है। इसलिये वह धरती की ही बातें करता है। जो स्वर्ग से उतरा है, सबके ऊपर है; ³²उसने जो कुछ देखा है, और सुना है, वह उसकी साक्षी देता है पर उसकी साक्षी को कोई ग्रहण नहीं करना चाहता। ³³जो उसकी साक्षी को मानता है वह प्रमाणित करता है कि परमेश्वर सच्चा है। ³⁴क्योंकि वह, जिसे परमेश्वर ने भेजा है, परमेश्वर की ही बातें बोलता है। क्योंकि परमेश्वर ने उसे आत्मा का अन्नत धन दिया है। ³⁵पिता अपने पुत्र को प्यार करता है। और उसी के हाथों